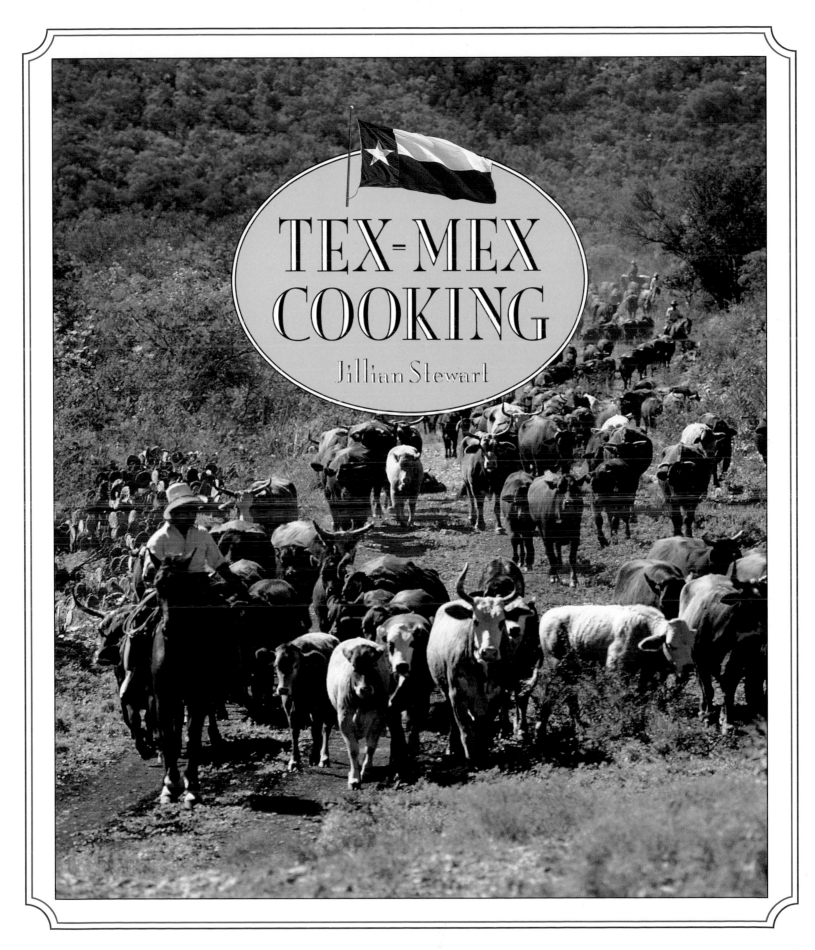

TEX-MEX COOKING

Jillian Stewart

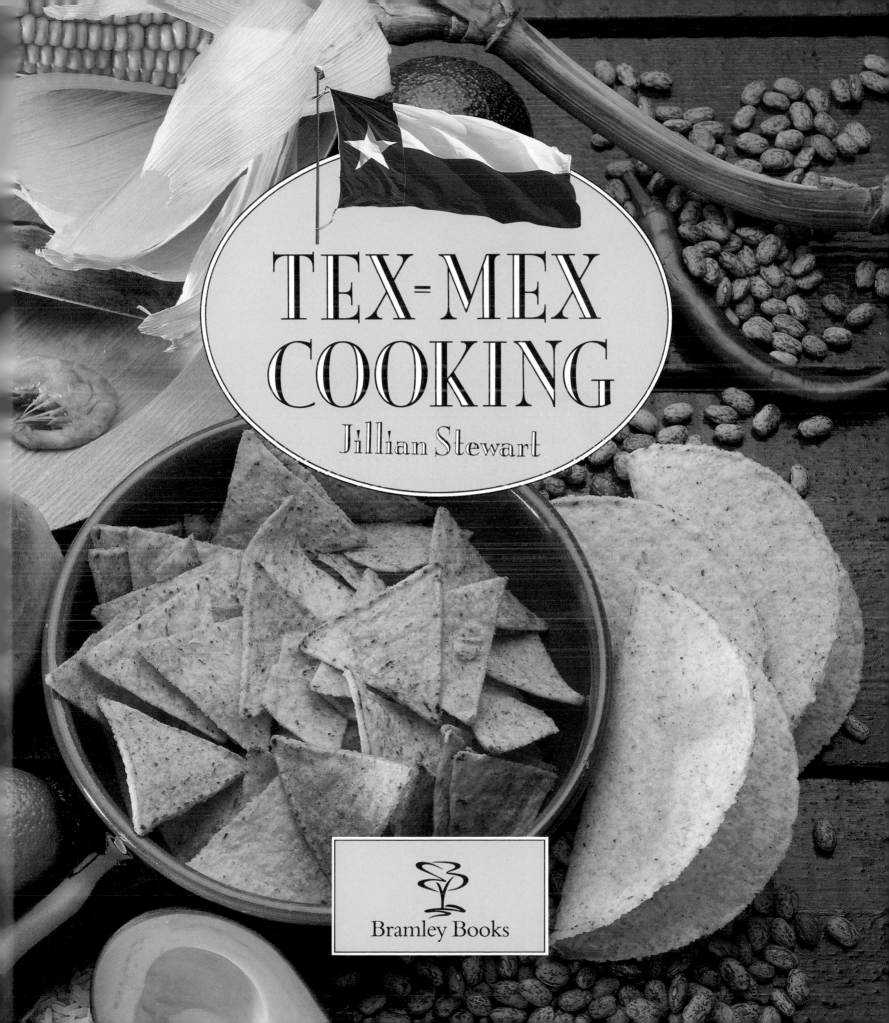

TEX-MEX COOKING

Jillian Stewart

Bramley Books

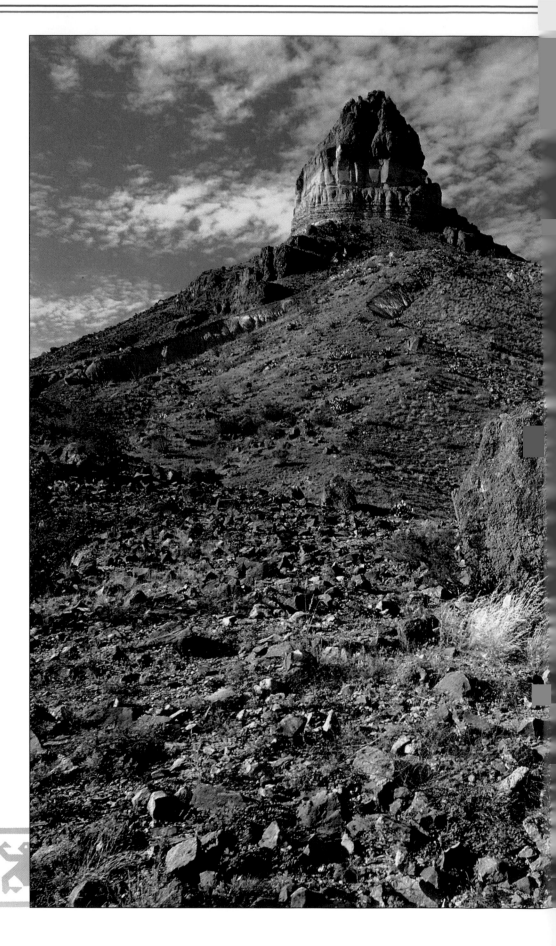

4172
This edition published in 1998 by Bramley Books
Copyright © 1994 Quadrillion Publishing Ltd
Godalming, Surrey GU7 1XW
All rights reserved
ISBN 1-85833-891-3

Editor: Jillian Stewart
Introduction: Bill Harris
Design: Philip Clucas
Picture research: Leora Kahn
Food photography: Neil Sutherland and
        Peter Barry
Typesetting: Inforum Ltd
Printed and bound in Singapore by Tien Wah Press

Contents

Introduction

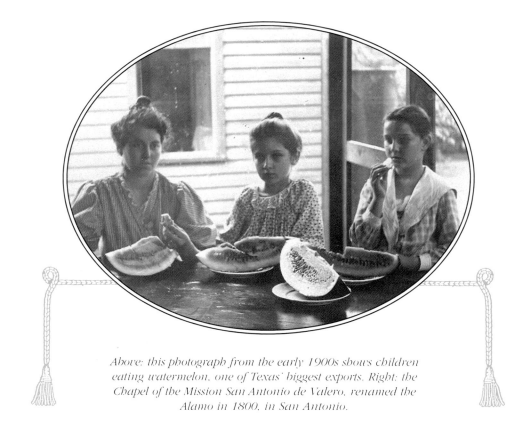

Above: this photograph from the early 1900s shows children eating watermelon. one of Texas' biggest exports. Right: the Chapel of the Mission San Antonio de Valero. renamed the Alamo in 1800. in San Antonio.

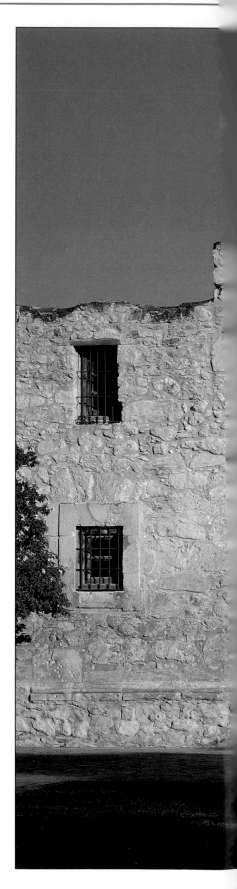

There is hardly a city anywhere these days that doesn't have at least one 'Tex-Mex' joint, where burritos and enchiladas often come from the same packet without regard for the fact that the former ought to be a filled flour tortilla and the latter made from a corn tortilla. The *pièce de résistance* in nearly all them is what they bill as Texas-style chilli, invariably made with hamburger meat, some canned tomatoes, kidney beans, reconstituted onions and prepackaged chilli powder. And many of those that have refried beans on their menus obviously get them from a can. The same is often true of the salsa.

But even though salsa in bottles and cans has replaced ketchup as the condiment of choice in many households, it may be as close as most of us will ever come to the real joy of border food, the first cousin of Mexican cuisine usually called Tex-Mex. But the

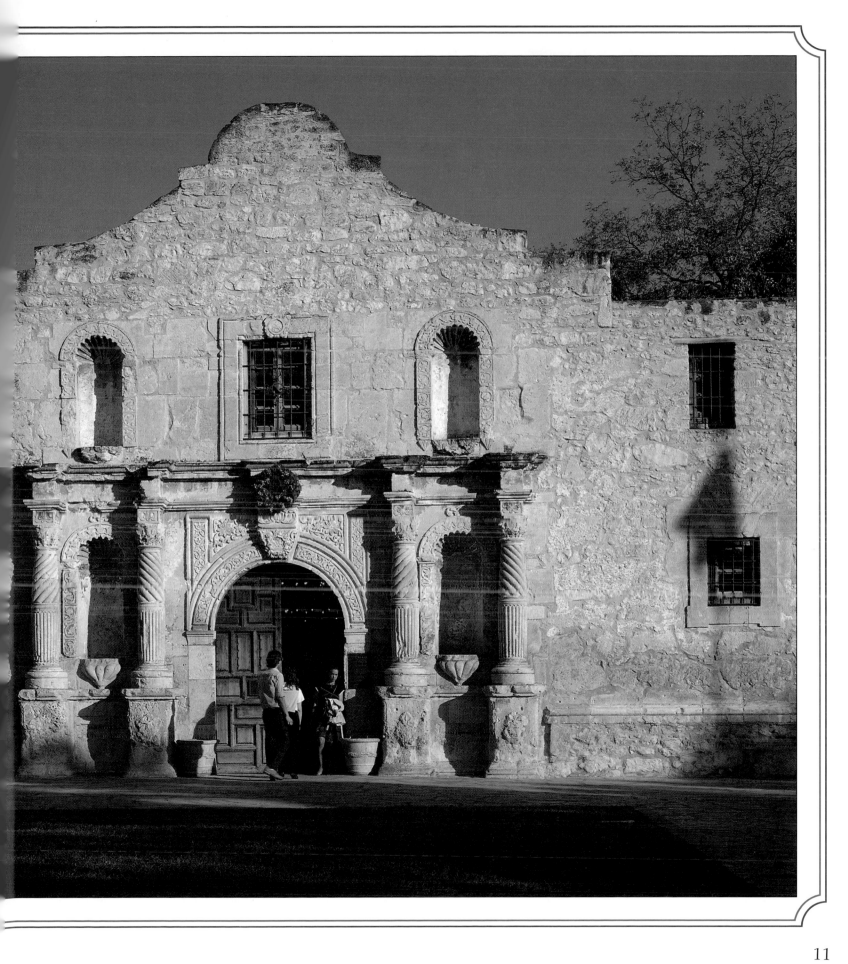

good news is that, although no one would ever regret having made the trip, it isn't necessary to go to Brownsville or El Paso to discover the pleasure. The fresh ingredients are available just about anywhere, and the bit of effort it takes to combine them quickly becomes a labour of love which, as any Texan will testify, is what makes all the difference.

Apart from loving care, what usually makes this cooking style memorable is the fruit of the plants of the genus *Capsicum,* whose 200 or more different varieties are known collectively as chillies. The word is used to describe the plant and its pods, but it also describes the classic dish made with chillies and meat, usually known in Texas as a 'bowl of red'. It is also a packaged powder made of chillies, cumin, oregano, salt and garlic usually laced with chemicals to extend its shelf life. Chillies themselves are also interchangeably called 'peppers', and we have Christopher Columbus to thank for that.

When he discovered the New World, the Admiral of the Ocean Sea set about naming some of the things he found. That he named the natives 'Indians' still raises hackles among the politically correct, but, then, Columbus never claimed to be an anthropologist. He apparently wasn't much of a botanist, either, because in his enthusiasm to prove that he had discovered the Indies, he decided that the chillies he found were a form of the plant that produces black pepper which, as it turns out, isn't even a close relative. It was a self-serving choice of words because back in the 15th century, black pepper was as valuable as gold and it was the prospect of finding a source of it that made funding his voyage seem like a good business proposition in the first place. But he might better have listened a little more closely to the people who met him at the shore. Their neighbours across the Gulf of Mexico, the Nahuatl, had been calling these pungent pods chilli for generations. Other pre-Columbian cultures had used them as commonly as modern cooks use salt for at least 5,000 years, possibly even longer. And along with corn and beans, chillies were among the first crops that turned prehistoric American hunters into farmers, bringing civilisation to the New World.

Chillies can be bought fresh or dried, frozen or canned, but they are also extremely easy to grow. Most varieties will thrive just about anywhere, even in a pot on a kitchen windowsill. It goes without saying that a little bit goes a long way and, once having introduced the plant into a garden, it is almost as adept at reseeding itself as hollyhocks. As 17th-century Americans grew tomatoes as decorative plants, some of their descendants do the same with chillies, almost all which are quite beautiful. But if they are a feast for the eyes, they also seem to be among the most healthy fruits available to mankind. They are unusually high in vitamins A, C and E, for instance, and as little as an ounce of chillies provides the recommended minimum daily requirement of all three. Added to this is a recent university study that concluded that chillies are a natural antibiotic whose germ-killing properties may be effective in curing colds and flu. The bottom line seems to be that these colourful pods are good for you. But even if they weren't, they do wonderful things to all kinds of food, turning almost any meal into an adventure and eliminating blandness from our culinary vocabulary.

The dominant characteristic of chillies is their heat, of course, but they also add flavour. Forgetting this, many cooks trying to avoid a palate-searing result sometimes opt for reducing the quantity of chillies called for in a recipe. They shouldn't, not only because it destroys the result by eliminating the important balance of flavour, but because there is a better way. The heat comes from a natural chemical called capsaicin that is generally concentrated in the seeds and the internal ribs of the chilli pod, and it can be dramatically reduced by cutting away those parts. Because the seeds and ribs are the source of the heat, it follows that the smaller the chilli the hotter it will be because of a greater concentration of capsaicin and a good rule of thumb to avoid excessive heat is to choose bigger chillies.

There are also ways to combat the heat in a chilli-laced dish. Down along the Rio Grande, folks will swear that a couple of long-necked bottles of beer will quench the fire, but the fact is that alcohol actually encourages the absorption of capsaicin and beer can make a fiery bowl of chilli seem even hotter. A better choice would be a glass of milk, which fights the fire, as do all dairy products, which explains why combination plates in most Tex-Mex restaurants, as well as many recipes, add a dollop of soured cream as a garnish. But if a glass of milk has a negative effect on an urban cowboy's image, starchy food can also neutralise the heat. Rice is a perfect choice, as any fan of fiery Szechuan Chinese food can tell you, but some crusty bread or even crackers can calm

Above: this illustration from 1874 shows a woman kneading tortillas in archetypal Mexican surroundings. A writer who visited the area at the time described the women as 'ceaselessly rolling out the tortilla, or frying it on the iron plate that sits over their bit of a fire.'

down any Tex-Mex dish, even one that would otherwise fog your glasses.

In many recipes, there is no substitute for fresh chillies, but if capsaicin can do strange things to your taste buds, it is also capable of burning your skin and calls for care in handling. Rubber gloves are always recommended while cutting away the seeds and veins, and special care should be taken not to touch your face and especially your eyes while handling the pods. And even though the rubber gloves have protected them, your hands should be thoroughly washed with hot soapy water after the job is done.

Dried chillies are useful in many Tex-Mex recipes because their flavours are more concentrated. If the pods aren't broken, they can be stored in covered containers for as long as six months, but before they are used, they need to be brought back to life. To do that, simply dry-roast them in a frying pan or in the oven for two or three minutes and then cover them with very hot, but not boiling, water for about twenty minutes more.

Like tomatoes and corn, the world knew nothing of chillies before the Spanish arrived in the Americas, but there is hardly a corner of the world where they aren't found today. And some cuisines are so centred on them, it is hard to imagine what people did for fun in the kitchen and dining room before the end of the 15th century. But there is another staple that Texas cooks have used for generations to add a special flavour to their barbecues and other grilled dishes that was largely a secret ingredient until a decade or so ago when restaurateurs throughout the United States began raising the level of border food to heights that had previously been restricted to the Southwest.

In some ways, it's strange the secret had been kept for so long. The Greeks had a word for it, 'prosopis', and in fact, botanists still call it that. The Aztecs, who used it liberally, called it 'mizquitl', which is the source of the modern American name, mesquite, the special wood whose smoke not only enhances the natural flavours of grilled food, but adds a subtle sweet flavour of its own not possible with any other kind of wood.

The mesquite tree is a perfect example of one of nature's creations that on first glance seems to have no other purpose than to harass man and beast, but turns out to be a great gift of nature once its orneriness are overlooked. In Texas, where it is known as switch mesquite, it is more bush than tree and it ranks among the ugliest denizens of the desert country. Its trunk is gnarled, its bark scaly, its branches twisted like a nest or serpents. The mesquite's leaves are feathery and might be called attractive, and even inviting on a hot summer day when they provide the only shade available, until you realise that they serve to camouflage the thorns underneath, some of which are as much as two inches long and all of them sharp as needles. It is the mortal enemy of other plants that share its space because even though it thrives in dry country, mesquite is one of the thirstiest plants alive. It isn't unusual for its main root to grow downward as far as two hundred feet in search of water and for the rest of its root system to radiate outward for sixty or seventy feet sucking every drop of moisture in its path. It is also one of the fastest-spreading of all trees and, once established, the hardest of all to eliminate. Cut down a mesquite tree and the roots will send up a couple of new shoots to replace it. And any rancher with money enough to dig up the roots finds it only a temporary solution because cattle consider mesquite seeds a kind of delicacy and because they are indigestible, the steers do a fine job of planting new trees. And to add insult to injury, in dry seasons when grass withers the mesquite produces more seed pods than in times when the grasses are lush, making them all the more attractive to hungry critters.

The wood was valuable to the early settlers in the Southwest for making fence posts, animal pens and small shelters but cowhands, who sneered at such things, found it perfect for cooking. Almost no other hardwood burns with a hotter flame and it ignites easily without any tinder, which is a boon for modern outdoor cooks who don't believe the fumes of petroleum-based lighter fuels add a thing to the flavour of their barbecue. Because mesquite coals are so much hotter, they sear food quickly and lock in the natural juices and, because the heat is longer-lasting, food is cooked more evenly. But the real advantage is mesquite's aroma, which enhances the flavour of beef as well as pork and game. In fact, just about anything cooked Tex-Mex style is better if it has been cooked over a mesquite fire.

Among those who would have said amen to that statement were the cowboys who led the great cattle drives northward from Texas in the years after the Civil War, or at least the men who drove the chuckwagons. Those cooks, always the most important men in any outfit after the trail boss himself, were probably the first to export border cooking north of the Red River and their lives weren't worth a thing if they didn't get it right. Among their duties was to move far ahead of the herd to select a perfect spot to make camp for the night, which meant that they were the first to run into trouble if there was any up ahead. But no matter what it took, they had to locate a campsite before the line of steers showed up on the horizon. It had to have water, of course, but more important was a stand of mesquite so they could get a hot fire going fast because as soon as the cattle were settled down, it would be time to eat, and no excuses were ever accepted. It was especially important when they got up at the crack of dawn to get the coffee made and to get the sourdough biscuits cooked. The latter were made in a dutch oven from starter the cooks prepared before they left Texas by mixing flour and salt together with water and storing it in a covered cask. It had to be kept warm all the way to Kansas, but if it couldn't be allowed to get

Above: an early photograph of two chefs from Waco, Texas.

chilled, it was also destroyed if it got too hot and either disaster was always lurking out there on the prairie. Although cowboys thrived on beef and beans, any cook who lost his stash of sourdough starter could probably expect to be forced to hit the trail on his own. Making the biscuits wasn't all that hard, all that was required was to put a bit of starter in the centre of the greased dutch oven, add some flour, salt, warm water and soda and then knead it until it felt just right. After that, all that was left to do was to put the dutch oven on the hot coals for a half hour or so, and add more flour, salt and warm water to the starter mixture in anticipation of the next day's breakfast. It was a simple process, but if the biscuits weren't perfect, it could not only ruin a cowpoke's day, but would guarantee a rough ride for the cook. Fortunately for many of them, their insistence on mesquite fires saved the hides of most of them. No wonder a good cook was paid $100 a month. He earned every penny. On the other hand, it should be noted that the average cowboy didn't believe that mesquite smoke did much to the trailside cuisine, and if they couldn't think of anything else to gripe about, the smoke could get them started. They had good reason to scorn the thorny bushes that their steers were forever wandering into, but they were usually too exhausted to notice any subtlety in their grub anyway. The bill of fare on a cattle drive consisted mostly of cooked pinto beans, coffee and those inevitable biscuits. Once in a while the monotony was broken with a pan-fried steak or a bowl of 'son-of-a-bitch stew', made from the intestines of nursing calves. The routine didn't vary at all for the three months it usually took to drive a herd from Texas up to Kansas and once the job was over and the cowboys were finished letting off a little steam, all they wanted was to get back to Texas and some of that good old down-home cooking.

During the years of the great cattle drives, the men who earned their living at it usually spent the off-season working at odd jobs, bragging about their exploits during the previous summer and arguing a lot among themselves. And chances are the thing they argued most about was what constituted a perfect bowl of chilli. Many Texans still do.

Just as many of them argue over whether it is barbecue or chilli that is the favourite food of the Lone Star State and even after the State Legislature came down on the side of chilli by voting it the state's official dish, the debate is still as fierce as ever. The barbecue partisans say their favourite dish should have won because the chilliheads can't even agree among themselves about how to make a perfect bowl of red. But in their official protest at the State House in Austin, they did admit it was so simple to make a pot of chilli that even little children could do it. 'The hardest thing about making chili', they said, 'is finding somebody to eat it'.

It was hitting below the belt, to be sure, and it wasn't long before the other camp countered the charge with figures to prove that chilli is to Texas what the potato was to the Irish, what pasta is to the Italians and rice to the Chinese. Nearly everyone involved had what they characterised as the perfect recipe for real Texas-style chilli, but as their neighbours on the barbecue side of the debate had pointed out in the first place, they couldn't agree about what was real and what wasn't.

The ensuing war led to a World Championship Chilli Cookoff at Terlinga, Texas, in 1966 and probably because it ended in a draw, it has become an annual event. And all over Texas these days, regional events are held to pick local champs to go on the the big one at Terlinga. Showmanship counts, of course, in the end cooking a pot of chilli is a serious business among the contestants. They get attention with such untraditional ingredients as rattlesnake meat, raccoon or armadillo and some even substitute chicken for meat. About the only thing they all agree on is that it is a sacrilege to add beans to anything described as chilli. Beyond that, it seems, anything goes. The day-long festivities include more than just cooking. They are marked with heavy-duty beer-drinking competitions, wet T-shirt contests, Wild West-style shootouts and some of the contests remembered from Sunday school picnics like egg-tossing, one-legged races and lemon rolls. But cooks with serious intentions of going on to Terlinga know that the basic rule of a good pot of chilli is to keep it simple. Most of the winning recipes have a thing or two in common: cubes of beef that have been marinated and browned, then seasoned with such things as coriander, cumin, garlic, oregano, paprika and crushed chillies. They almost never contain onions, tomatoes or bell peppers and never, ever, beans. The binding ingredient is masa harina, a dough made from ground dried corn. The rest is whatever the cook decides it takes to make a perfect bowl of red. And as in all Tex-Mex cooking it is a combination of imagination and tender loving care.

But Tex Mex food, as you are about to discover for yourself, is more than a memorable barbecue or a perfect bowl of red. Its hallmark is a studied lack of pretense, and although modern Texans are comfortable in Continental style restaurants, they are at their most contented when the accent is homey. They've tasted caviar, but prefer pickled black-eyed peas. They are as willing to try new ideas as any other Americans, but in the end, the ones that stay with them are the ones that fit best with the ideas of their ancestors. It is why the flavour of Texas isn't likely to change any time soon. And why so much of the rest of the country is running to catch up.

CHAPTER ONE
Soups and Appetizers

Above: the ghost town of Terlingua was once a city of over 2,000 which sprang up following the discovery of mercury in 1890.

*T*he varied cuisine that comes together under the banner of Tex-Mex cooking is succinctly reflected in the variety of its soups and appetizers. The traditional ingredients of Southwestern cooking – beef, chillies, corn and avocados – recur in many dishes, but in a variety of combinations. One of the most popular appetizers is, of course, guacamole, but not to be missed are the many delicious, hearty soups. These reflect the cowboy's love of filling dishes and the enduring popularity of soups south of the border. Delicious, heart-warming soups are ubiquitous in Mexico and feature a variety of ingredients, from beef or pork with onion and garlic and a purée of tomatoes, to zesty seafood chowders flavoured with lime.

Chilli Vegetable Soup

Cornmeal Pancakes

Cornmeal, either yellow, white or blue, is an important ingredient in Tex-Mex recipes. Here it's combined with corn to make a light appetizer; the pancakes can also be served as a side dish to a main course.

150g/5oz yellow cornmeal
1 tbsp flour
1 tsp baking powder
1 tsp salt
2 eggs, separated
460ml/16 fl oz buttermilk
Oil
280g/10oz frozen corn
Soured cream
Red pepper preserves
Spring onions, chopped

Sift the dry ingredients into a bowl, adding any coarse meal that remains in the strainer. Mix the egg yolks and buttermilk together and gradually beat into the dry ingredients. Cover and leave to stand for at least 15 minutes. Whisk the egg whites until stiff, but not dry, and fold into the cornmeal mixture. Lightly grease a frying pan with oil and drop in about 2 tablespoons of batter. Sprinkle with the corn and allow to cook until the underside is golden brown. Turn

Chillies and lime juice give this soup the startling sharp flavours so typical of Tex-Mex cooking.

1 tbsp oil
1 onion, chopped
120g/4oz canned whole green chillies, quartered
1.1 litres/2 pints chicken stock
1 large potato, peeled and cut into short strips
Full quantity Taco Sauce recipe (see page 30)
1 tbsp lime juice
Salt
Tortilla chips and lime slices, to garnish

Heat the oil in a large saucepan and sauté the onion until translucent. Add the green chillies, stock, potato and taco sauce. Cover the pan and simmer for 20 minutes. Stir in the lime juice and add salt. Serve in individual bowls with tortilla chips. Cut a thin slice of lime to float in each bowl of soup. Serves 4.

the pancakes and cook the second side until golden. Continue with the remaining batter and corn. Keep the cooked pancakes warm. To serve, place three pancakes on warm side plates. Add a spoonful of soured cream and red pepper preserves to each and sprinkle with finely sliced or shredded spring onions. Serves 4.

Above left: the cowboy's basic diet has altered surprisingly little in the last century; it is the hearty combination of beans, meat, biscuits and coffee that still provide sustenance.

Beef & Bean Soup

The use of the Tex-Mex speciality of refried beans in this recipe has the dual purpose of adding local flavour and thickening this hearty soup. Cumin, cinnamon and cayenne are all strong components of the Tex-Mex character.

1 large onion, finely chopped
1 red pepper, finely chopped
2 sticks celery, chopped
2 tbsps oil
225g/8oz ground beef
6 tomatoes, peeled, seeded and chopped
420g/15oz canned refried beans
1 tsp ground cumin
1 tsp chilli powder
Pinch of cinnamon and cayenne pepper
1 tsp garlic powder or purée
Salt and pepper
570ml/1 pint beef stock

Fry the onion, pepper and celery in the oil in a large saucepan until softened. Add the beef and fry over medium heat until well browned. Add the tomatoes and refried beans with the spices, garlic and seasoning and mix well. Stir in the stock and bring to the boil. Cover and simmer gently for 30 minutes, stirring occasionally. Pour the soup into a blender or food processor and purée. The soup will be quite thick and not completely smooth. Adjust the seasoning and serve with tortilla chips. Top with soured cream if desired. Serves 4.

Prawns Acapulco

These prawns laced with Tex-Mex spices make an exciting appetizer.

4 slices bread, crusts removed
90g/3oz softened butter
180g/6oz cooked and peeled prawns
½ tsp chilli powder
¼ tsp paprika
¼ tsp cumin
Salt and pepper
Watercress, to garnish

Cut the bread slices in half and spread with 2 tablespoons of the butter. Butter both sides sparingly. Place the bread on a baking sheet and cook in a preheated 180°C/350°F/Gas Mark 4 oven for 10-15 minutes until golden brown. Keep warm. Melt the remaining butter in a small pan and add the prawns, spices and seasoning and stir well. Heat through completely and spoon on top of the bread slices. Garnish with watercress and serve hot. Serves 4.

Above left: this early photograph shows a family preparing to take their produce to market.

Guacamole

It is essential for the Tex-Mex cook to have guacamole in his or her repertoire. It is commonly served as a dip with tortilla chips, as a side-dish to be eaten with barbecued meats and chillies or it is piled onto and into many of those wrapped-up Tex-Mex specialities such as flautas, chimichangas and enchiladas.

1 medium onion, finely chopped
1 clove garlic, crushed
Grated rind and juice of ½ lime
½ quantity Taco Sauce recipe (see page 30)
3 large avocados
Pinch of salt
1 tbsp chopped fresh coriander
Coriander leaves, to garnish

Mix the onion, garlic, rind and juice of lime and the taco sauce together in a large mixing bowl. Cut the avocados in half lengthways. Twist the halves gently in opposite directions to separate. Hit the stone with a large, sharp knife and twist the embedded knife to remove the stone. Place the avocado halves cut side down on a chopping board. Lightly score the skin lengthways and gently pull back to peel. Alternatively, scoop out avocado flesh with a spoon, scraping the skin well. Chop the avocado roughly and immediately place in the bowl with the onion and lime. Use a potato masher to break up the avocado until almost smooth. Do not over-mash. Season with salt and stir in the chopped coriander. Spoon into a serving bowl and garnish with coriander leaves. Serves 8 as a dip.

Above right: Palo Duro Canyon in Texas has been carved over millions of years by the flow of the Red River and the erosive action of wind and rain. Below: the old Spanish church of Mission San José, San Antonio.

CHAPTER TWO
Tortillas and Turnovers

Above: a 19th-century engraving shows women preparing tortillas in the traditional manner.

A *favourite part of many Tex-Mex meals are the myriad varieties of delicious stuffed tortillas. Packed with anything from spicy ground beef to vegetables and refried beans, these mouthwatering parcels of Tex-Mex flavour owe much to the street food of Mexico. Here, tortillas are wrapped around a filling and sold on the streets and in the markets as a convenient ready-to-eat snack. Tex-Mex versions tend to be larger and a little less easy to eat than their Mexican counterparts, but they taste just as divine. The great attraction of filled tortillas is their adaptability; almost any ingredient can be used as a filling and combined with sauces, toppings and salads to give a dish that is as individual as its creator!*

Tortillas

Flautas

Flautas, literally flutes, are double length stuffed tortillas. Tex-Mex style would be to eat them with rice, refried beans and a tomato and avocado salad.

1 tbsp oil
225g/8oz chicken, skinned, boned and ground or finely chopped
1 small onion, finely chopped
½ green pepper, finely chopped
½-1 chilli, seeded and finely chopped
90g/3oz frozen corn
6 black olives, pitted and chopped
120ml/4 fl oz double cream
Salt
12 prepared tortillas (see page 26)
Taco sauce (see page 30), guacamole and soured cream for toppings

Heat the oil in a medium frying pan and add the chicken, onion and pepper. Cook over moderate heat, stirring frequently to break up the pieces of chicken. When the chicken is cooked and the vegetables are softened, add the chilli, corn, olives, cream and salt. Bring to the boil and boil rapidly, stirring continuously, to reduce and thicken the cream. Place 2

Borrowed from Mexico, these have become indispensible in Tex-Mex cooking and are used as a base for tacos, enchiladas and other Tex-Mex dishes. In Mexico the tortilla is made from lime-soaked dried corn, which is soaked and ground into a dough called masa. Here, flour is used.

225g/8oz plain flour (more if necessary)
2 tsps baking powder
Pinch of salt
60g/2oz white cooking fat
120-200ml/4-7 fl oz hot water
Oil for frying

Sift the flour, baking powder and salt into a bowl. Rub in the vegetable shortening until the mixture resembles coarse crumbs. Add water, mixing until absorbed. Knead gently and add more flour if the dough is too sticky. Cover and leave to rest for 15 minutes. Divide the dough into ten even-sized pieces. Roll into balls on a floured surface, cover and leave to stand for 20 minutes. Roll out each ball on a lightly floured surface to a circle 18cm/7 inches in diameter. Cover the finished tortillas while rolling all the remaining dough. Place a lightly oiled frying pan over high heat. Fry the tortillas individually on both sides until bubbles form on the surface. Stack them as they are cooked and set them aside until ready to use. Makes 12.

tortillas side by side on a clean work surface, overlapping them by about 5cm/2 inches. Spoon some of the chicken mixture in a line across the middle of the 2 tortillas, roll up the 2 together and secure with cocktail sticks. Fry each flauta in about 1cm/½-inch oil. Do not allow them to get very brown. Drain on kitchen towels. Arrange flautas on serving plates and top with soured cream, guacamole and taco sauce. Serves 6.

Right: this fascinating photograph, dating from 1904, shows children enjoying making tortillas with their maid. Above left: The Ranching Heritage Center in Lubbock contains a variety of relocated and restored ranching structures.

Tacos

This is one of the classic mainstays of Tex-Mex cooking. It always looks impressive when served at home and is easily made with packaged taco shells. A good tip is to place the empty taco shells on their open ends when warming to keep them from closing up, so making filling easier.

12 taco shells

BEEF FILLING	TOPPINGS
1 tbsp oil	Shredded lettuce
450g/1lb ground beef	Grated cheese
1 medium onion, chopped	Tomatoes, seeded and chopped
2 tsps ground cumin	Chopped spring onions
1 clove garlic, crushed	Avocado slices
2 tsps chilli powder	Soured cream
Pinch of paprika	Jalapeño peppers
Salt and pepper	Taco Sauce (see page 30)

CHICKEN FILLING
45g/1½oz butter or margarine
1 medium onion, chopped
1 small red pepper, chopped
2 tbsps flaked almonds
340g/12oz chicken breasts, skinned and finely chopped
Salt and pepper
1 piece fresh root ginger, peeled and chopped
90ml/3 fl oz milk
2 tsps cornflour
140ml/¼ pint soured cream

Heat oil for beef filling in a large frying pan and brown the beef and onion, breaking the meat up with a fork as it cooks. Add spices, garlic and seasoning and cook about 20 minutes. Set aside.

For the chicken filling, melt 2 tablespoons butter or margarine in a medium saucepan and add the onion. Cook slowly until softened. Add the pepper and almonds and cook slowly until the almonds are lightly browned. Stir often during cooking. Remove to a plate and set aside. Melt the remaining butter in the same saucepan and cook the chicken for about 5 minutes, turning frequently. Season and return the onion mixture to the pan along with the chopped ginger. Blend milk and cornflour and stir into the chicken mixture. Bring to the boil and stir until very thick. Mix in the soured cream and cook gently to heat through. Do not boil.

Heat the taco shells on a baking sheet in a preheated 180°C/350°F/Gas Mark 4 oven for 2-3 minutes. Place on the sheet with the open ends down. To fill, hold the shell in one hand, and spoon in about 1 tablespoon of either beef or chicken filling. Next, add a layer of shredded lettuce, followed by a layer of grated cheese. Add choice of other toppings and finally spoon on some taco sauce. Serves 6.

Above: rounding up the horses on a Texan ranch. Although there are fewer cowboys in Texas these days, they still run their longhorns through Texas' wide open spaces.

Taco Sauce

This basic recipe can be used as a sauce or topping for fish, meat or poultry main dishes. It is also found in tacos, tostadas and nachos, and is used as a dip for tortilla chips or vegetable crudités.

Gulf Coast Tacos

This authentic recipe uses tomatillos and jicama root – both of which can be difficult to find. If unavailable, substitute one large green tomato for the tomatillos and a small can of water chestnuts for the jicama.

6 Tortillas (see page 26)

GREEN CHILLI SALSA
1 tbsp oil
3 tomatillos, husks removed
1 clove garlic
30g/1oz coriander leaves
2 green chillies
Juice of 1 lime
140ml/¼ pint soured cream
Pinch of salt and sugar

FILLING INGREDIENTS
225g/8oz large raw prawns, peeled
225g/8oz raw scallops, quartered if large
1 tsp coriander seed, crushed
1 shallot, finely chopped
Salt and pepper
90ml/3 fl oz white wine
1 small jicama root, peeled and cut into thin matchstick strips
Coriander leaves and lime wedges

Prepare the Tortillas according to the recipe. Heat the oil for the salsa,

1 tbsp oil
1 onion, diced
1 green pepper, diced
½-1 red or green chilli
½ tsp ground cumin
½ tsp ground coriander
½ clove garlic, crushed
Pinch of salt, pepper and sugar
400g/4oz canned tomatoes
Tomato purée (optional)

Heat the oil in a heavy-based saucepan and when hot, add the onion and pepper. Cook slowly to soften slightly. Chop the chilli and add with the cumin, coriander and garlic and cook a further 2-3 minutes. Add sugar, seasonings and tomatoes with their juice. Break up the tomatoes with a fork or a potato masher. Cook a further 5-6 minutes over moderate heat to reduce and thicken slightly. Add tomato purée for colour, if necessary. Adjust seasoning and use hot or cold according to your recipe. Makes 280ml/½ pint.

slice the tomatillos and sauté them for about 3 minutes. Place in a food processor along with the garlic, coriander, chillies and lime juice. Purée until smooth. Fold in the soured cream, season and chill. Heat oil in a deep sauté pan to a depth of at least 5cm/2 inches. When hot, add a tortilla and press down under the oil with a metal spoon. When the tortilla starts to puff up, take it out and fold in half to form a shell. Hold in shape until it cools slightly and sets. Repeat with the remaining tortillas. Keep them warm in an oven, standing on their open ends to prevent them closing.
Place the prawns, scallops, coriander seeds, shallot and salt and pepper in a frying pan with the wine and water to barely cover. Cook for about 8 minutes, stirring occasionally, until the seafood is cooked. Fill the taco shells with the jicama. Remove the seafood from the liquid and arrange on top of the jicama. Top with the salsa and garnish with coriander leaves. Serve with lime wedges. Serves 6.

Above left: preparing a meal outside a Mexican jacal – a traditional hut made of wooden planks and straw or rushes.

Enchiladas

Sauces and fillings for enchiladas, a Mexican speciality brought into the Tex-Mex fold, can be infinitely varied to suit individual tastes.

12 Tortillas (see page 26)
90g/3oz grated cheese
Sliced spring onions, to garnish

SAUCE
10 ripe tomatoes, peeled, seeded and chopped
1 small onion, chopped
1-2 tbsps tomato purée
1-2 green or red chillies, seeded and chopped
1 clove garlic, crushed
Salt
Pinch of sugar
30g/1oz butter or margarine
2 eggs
280ml/½ double cream

MEAT FILLING
340g/12oz ground pork
1 small red pepper, chopped
4 tbsps raisins
4 tbsps pine nuts
Salt and pepper

To make sauce, place tomatoes, onion, tomato purée, chillies, garlic, salt and sugar in a blender or food processor and purée until smooth. Melt butter or margarine in a large saucepan. Add the tomato mixture and simmer for 5 minutes. Beat together the eggs and cream, mixing well. Add a spoonful of the hot tomato mixture to the cream and eggs and mix quickly. Return this to the saucepan with the rest of the tomato mixture. Heat slowly, stirring constantly, until the mixture thickens. Do not boil.

Meanwhile, cook the pork and pepper slowly in a large frying pan. Use a fork to break up the meat as it cooks. Turn up the heat when the pork is nearly cooked and fry briskly for a few minutes. Add the raisins, pine nuts and seasoning. Combine about ¼ of the sauce with the meat and divide mixture evenly among all the tortillas. Spoon the filling onto one side of the centre and roll up the tortilla around it, leaving the ends open and some of the filling showing. Place enchiladas seam side down in a baking dish and pour over the remaining sauce, leaving the ends uncovered. Sprinkle over the cheese and bake in a preheated 180° C/350° F/Gas Mark 4 oven for 15-20 minutes, or until the sauce begins to bubble. Sprinkle with the sliced onions and serve immediately. Serves 6.

Above: the state flower of Texas, the bluebonnet. There are more than 5,000 different kinds of flower in the Lone Star State, but the bluebonnet is among the most beautiful.

Chalupas

These are tortillas in another form, this time a snack with spicy meat. For a main course, add Refried Beans or Spicy Rice and Beans as an accompaniment.

½ quantity Tortilla recipe (see page 26)
Oil, for frying
Full quantity Red Sauce (see recipe for Southwestern Stir-fry, page 52)
340g/12oz ground beef
2 cloves garlic, crushed
1 tsp dried oregano
2 tsps cumin
Salt and pepper
90g/3oz frozen corn
4 tbsps raisins

TOPPINGS
6-8 spring onions, chopped
4-6 tomatoes, diced
½ a small head lettuce, shredded
140ml/¼ pint soured cream
120g/4oz grated cheese

Prepare the tortillas according to the recipe and divide the dough in 10. After the required resting time, roll the balls of dough into 9cm/3½-inch rounds. Prepare the red sauce according to the recipe instructions and set it aside. Heat at least 5cm/2 inches of oil in a frying pan. When hot, place in one tortilla at a time and fry briefly until just crisp. Drain and keep them warm. Cook the beef slowly in a large frying pan until the fat begins to render. Add the garlic, oregano and cumin and raise the heat to brown the meat. Season to taste and then stir in enough of the red sauce to moisten the meat well. Add the corn and raisins, cover the pan and leave to stand for 5 minutes. Spoon the meat onto the tortillas and drizzle over more sauce. Garnish with your choice of toppings.

Chimichangas

Chimichangas are delicious deep-fried tortilla parcels containing chilli, onions and cheese. A Tex-Mex meal would feature them as an appetizer or a main course served with rice and refried beans.

6 flour tortillas (see page 26)
½ quantity Chilli con Carne recipe (see page 54)
6 lettuce leaves, shredded
6 spring onions, chopped
3oz Cheddar cheese, grated
Oil for frying
½ quantity Guacamole recipe (see page 22)
140ml/¼ pint soured cream
1 tomato, seeded and chopped

Wrap the tortillas in foil and place in a warm oven for 5 minutes to make them pliable. Heat the chilli briefly and spoon about 2 tablespoons onto the centre of each tortilla. Top with lettuce, onions and cheese. Fold in the sides to make a parcel, making sure all the filling is enclosed. Heat about 2.5cm/1 inch of oil in a large sauté pan and when hot lower in the chimichangas, folded side down first. Cook 2-4 at a time depending on the size of the pan. Cook for 3

minutes and carefully turn over. Cook a further 3 minutes and remove to kitchen towels and drain. Repeat with remaining chimichangas. Spoon the guacamole over the top of each and drizzle over the soured cream. Sprinkle over the chopped tomato and serve immediately. Serves 6 as an appetizer, or 3 as a main course.

Above: an illustration from 1878 of Mexican women making frijoles in a rural kitchen in the Tierras Calientes.

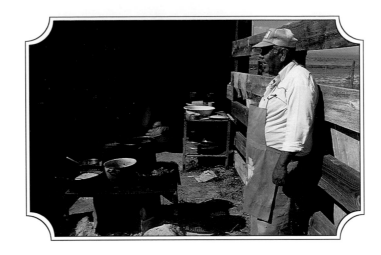

Burritos

The name is Spanish for 'little donkeys' and the dish is a very popular one. Beans are the traditional filling, but meat may be used as well. Burritos can be served as an appetizer or as a main course with rice and guacamole.

6 flour tortillas (see page 26)
1 onion, chopped
1 tbsp oil
450g/1lb canned refried beans
6 lettuce leaves, shredded
120g/4oz Cheddar cheese, grated
2 tomatoes, sliced
2 tbsps snipped chives
Full quantity Taco Sauce recipe (see page 30)
140ml/¼ pint soured cream
Chopped coriander leaves

Wrap tortillas in foil and heat in a warm oven to soften. Cook the onion in the oil until soft but not coloured. Add the beans and heat through. Spoon the mixture down the centre of each tortilla. Top with lettuce, cheese, tomatoes and chives. Fold over the sides to form long rectangular parcel. Make sure the filling is completely enclosed. Place burritos in an ovenproof dish, cover and cook in a preheated 180° C/350° F/Gas Mark 4 oven for about 20 minutes. Spoon over the taco sauce. Top with soured cream and sprinkle with chopped coriander to serve.
Serves 6 as an appetizer.

Empanadas

This is a Tex-Mex recipe that has been adapted from the Spanish pastries popular in Mexico.

Triple quantity pastry recipe from Chilli Prawn Quiche (see page 46)
1 egg

FILLING
1 onion, chopped
1 clove garlic, finely chopped
1 small green pepper, chopped
1 tbsp oil
225g/8oz ground beef
1 tsp cocoa powder
1 tbsp flour
½ tsp ground cumin
½ tsp paprika
½ tsp dried oregano, crushed
Salt and pepper
1-2 chillies, seeded and chopped
2 tbsps tomato purée
3 tbsps water
2 tbsps flaked almonds
2 tbsps raisins

Prepare the pastry according to the recipe for Chilli Prawn Quiche. Cook the onion, garlic and pepper in the oil in a frying pan until soft but not coloured. Add the meat and fry quickly until well browned. Add the cocoa, flour, spices, oregano and seasonings. Stir well and cook briefly before adding the chillies, tomato purée and water. Cook slowly for 10-15 minutes. Add nuts and raisins and allow to cool. Roll out the pastry on a floured surface and cut out 6 rounds using a 15cm/6-inch plate as a guide. Place the cooled filling on one side of the rounds of pastry and dampen the edges with water. Fold over and press to seal the edges. Crimp the edges if desired. Place on baking sheets and brush with a mixture of beaten egg and salt. Make sure the egg glaze is brushed on evenly. Prick once or twice with a fork and bake in a 220° C/425° F/Gas Mark 7 oven for about 15 minutes, or until golden brown. Makes 6.

CHAPTER THREE
Fish and Seafood

Above: comancheros in Josie's Gaslight Square, Corpus Christi.

*T*he growth of interest in healthy eating has heralded a welcome growth in the popularity of Tex-Mex seafood dishes. The gulf waters provide an abundance of fresh delights, from sparkling prawns, to red snapper and swordfish, while the area's rivers provide such favourites as bass, trout and catfish. A wonderfully adaptable ingredient, seafood is served up in numerous exciting ways. Prawns are combined with a spicy taco sauce, while freshwater fish is often coated in a spicy cornmeal and served with lime wedges. Undoubtedly Tex-Mex cuisine owes a great debt of gratitude to the native Americans who showed the way in utilising local produce, from brook trout to the ubiquitous corn, to create a regional cuisine that is uniquely diverse.

Swordfish with Grapefruit Tequila Salsa

Swordfish from the Gulf of Mexico spiked with the tart flavours of local citrus fruits and tequila – the liquor distilled from the Peyote cactus – makes a true Tex-Mex delicacy. For extra flavour, and to enrich the fish, the swordfish steaks may be marinated in a lime juice and oil mixture for up to an hour beforehand.

4-6 ruby or pink grapefruit (depending on size)
1 lime
½ green chilli, seeded and finely diced
1 spring onion, finely chopped
2 tbsps chopped fresh coriander
1 tbsp sugar
3 tbsps tequila
Juice of 1 lime
2 tbsps oil
Black pepper, to taste
4-8 swordfish steaks (depending on size)
Coriander sprigs for garnish

Remove the zest from the grapefruit and lime with a zester and set it aside. Remove all the pith from the

Prawns Veracruz

Veracruz is a port on the Gulf of Mexico which lends its name to this colourful seafood Tex-Mex dish.

1 tbsp oil
1 onion, chopped
1 large green pepper, cut into short strips
2-3 green chillies, seeded and chopped
Double quantity Taco Sauce recipe (see page 30)
2 tomatoes, peeled and chopped
12 pimiento-stuffed olives, halved
2 tsps capers
¼ tsp ground cumin
Salt
450g/1lb prawns, uncooked
Juice of 1 lime

Heat the oil in a large frying pan and add the onion and pepper. Cook until soft but not coloured. Add chillies, taco sauce, tomatoes, olives, capers, cumin and salt. Bring to the boil and then lower the heat to simmer for 5 minutes. Remove black veins, if present, from the rounded side of the prawns. Add the prawns to the sauce and cook until they curl up and turn pink and opaque. Add the lime juice to taste and serve. Serves 6.

grapefruit and segment them. Squeeze the lime for juice. Mix the grapefruit and citrus zests with the chilli, onion, coriander, sugar, tequila and lime juice and set aside. Mix remaining lime juice, oil and pepper together and brush both sides of the fish. Place under a pre-heated grill and cook for about 4 minutes each side depending on distance from the heat source. To serve, place a coriander sprig on each fish steak and serve with the grapefruit salsa. Serves 4.

Above left: Harrell House in Lubbock's Ranching Heritage Center is the perfect example of a ranch home at the end of the nineteenth century.

Plaice with Spicy Tomato Sauce

With Mexico and Texas both bordering the Gulf of Mexico it's logical that Tex-Mex cooking should incorporate fish into its repertoire.

90g/3oz cream cheese
1 tsp dried oregano
Pinch of cayenne pepper
4 whole fillets of plaice
Lime slices and dill, to garnish

TOMATO SAUCE
1 tbsp oil
1 small onion, chopped
1 stick celery, chopped
1 chilli, seeded and chopped
¼ tsp each ground cumin, coriander and ginger
½ red and ½ green pepper, chopped
400g/14oz canned tomatoes
1 tbsp tomato purée
Salt, pepper and a pinch sugar

To prepare the sauce, heat the oil in a heavy-based pan and cook the onion, celery, chilli and spices for about 5 minutes over very low heat. Add the peppers and the remaining sauce ingredients and bring to the boil. Reduce heat and simmer 15-20 minutes, stirring occasionally. Set aside while preparing the fish. Mix the cream cheese, oregano and cayenne pepper together and set aside. Skin the fillets using a filleting knife. Start at the tail end and hold the knife at a slight angle to the skin. Push the knife along using a sawing motion, with the blade against the skin. Dip fingers in salt to make it easier to hold onto the fish skin. Gradually separate the fish from the skin. Spread the cheese filling on all 4 fillets and roll each up. Secure with cocktail sticks. Place the fillets in a lightly greased baking dish, cover and cook for 10 minutes in a preheated 180° C/350° F/Gas Mark 4 oven. Pour over the tomato sauce and cook a further 10-15 minutes. Fish is cooked when it feels firm and looks opaque. Garnish with lime slices and dill. Serves 4.

Above: the mountains of Big Bend National Park.
Right: a shrimp boat, in the Port of Galveston.

Fried Bass in Cornmeal

Corn, the staple of the aboriginal peoples of the USA and Mexico, was adopted by the New World settlers. It continues to be the mainstay of Tex-Mex cooking, not only as the basis of tortilla dough but also as a crisp and subtly-flavoured coating for fried foods. For extra Tex-Mex taste serve this bass with red chilli preserves or relish.

280g/10oz yellow cornmeal
2 tbsps flour
Pinch of salt
2 tsps cayenne pepper
1 tsp ground cumin
2 tsps garlic granules
900g/2lbs freshwater bass or other whitefish fillets
Milk
Oil for deep frying
Lime wedges, to garnish

Mix the cornmeal, flour, salt, cayenne, cumin and garlic together in a shallow container or on a piece of greaseproof paper. Skin the fillets if desired. Dip them into the milk and then lift to allow the excess to drip off. Place the fish in the cornmeal mixture and turn to coat the fish completely. Meanwhile, heat oil in a deep frying pan, large saucepan or deep-fat fryer. Add the fish in small batches and cook until the fillets float to the surface. Turn over and cook to brown lightly and evenly. Drain on kitchen towels and serve immediately with lime wedges.
Serves 4.

Above left: the Rio Grande has carved a unique landscape in Big Bend National Park.
Left: the paddle-wheeler Colonel, moored in the Port of Galveston.

Chilli Prawn Quiche

Chillies, spring onions and garlic give this prawn quiche Tex-Mex bite and flavour.

PASTRY
120g/4oz plain flour
30g/1oz butter or margarine
2 tbsps white cooking fat
2-4 tbsps cold water

FILLING
4 eggs
140ml/¼ pint milk
140ml/¼ pint cream
½ clove garlic, crushed
Salt
120g/4oz Cheddar cheese, grated
3 spring onions, chopped
2 green chillies, seeded and chopped
225g/8oz cooked and peeled prawns
Salt
Cooked, unpeeled prawns for garnish

Sift the flour with a pinch of salt into a mixing bowl, or place in a food processor and mix once or twice. Rub in the butter and fat until the mixture resembles fine breadcrumbs, or work in the food processor, being careful not to over-mix. Mix in the liquid gradually, adding enough to bring the pastry together in a ball. In a food processor, add the liquid through the funnel while
the machine is running. Wrap the pastry well and chill for 20-30 minutes.
Roll out the pastry on a well-floured surface with a floured rolling pin. Wrap the circle of pastry around the rolling pin to lift it into a 25cm/10-inch pie dish. Unroll the pastry over the pan. Carefully press it onto the bottom and up the sides of the pan, taking care not to stretch it. Roll the rolling pin over the top of the dish to remove excess pastry, or cut off with a sharp knife.
Mix the eggs, milk, cream and garlic together. Add salt. Sprinkle the cheese, onions, chillies and prawns onto the base of the pastry and pour over the egg mixture. Bake in a preheated 200° C/400° F/Gas Mark 6 oven for 30-40 minutes until firm and golden brown. Peel the tail shells off the prawns and remove the legs and roe if present. Use prawns to garnish the quiche. Serves 6.

Above: this fascinating photograph from the late 1800s shows a chilli stand on the east side of Military Plaza, San Antonio.

46

Riverside Trout

In Tex-Mex cooking fried foods are coated in corn, the indigenous staple grain. Fish dredged in cornmeal is deliciously crisp and sealed. It must, however, be dipped in the cornmeal just before cooking. If it is allowed to stand, the result will be soggy.

90-120ml/3-4 fl oz vegetable oil
4 tbsps pine nuts
8 rashers bacon, diced
150g/5oz yellow cornmeal
Pinch salt and white pepper
4 trout weighing about 225g/8oz each, cleaned
Juice of 1 lime
Fresh sage

Above left: an engraving from 1854 of a Mexican inn. Below: the stunning scenery and impressive waters of the Rio Grande.

*Heat 90ml/3 fl oz of the oil in a large frying pan. Add the pine nuts and cook over moderate heat, stirring constantly. When a pale golden brown, remove them and drain on kitchen towels. Add the bacon to the oil and cook until crisp, stirring constantly. Drain with the pine nuts. Mix the cornmeal, salt and pepper, and dredge the fish well, patting on the cornmeal. Shake off any excess. If necessary, add more oil to the pan – it should come about halfway up the sides of the fish. Re-heat over moderately high heat. When hot, add the fish two at a time and fry until golden brown, about 4-5 minutes. Turn over, reduce the heat slightly if necessary and cook a further 4-5 minutes. Drain and repeat with the remaining fish. Drain almost all the oil from the pan and re-heat the bacon and nuts very briefly. Add the lime juice and cook a few seconds. Spoon the bacon and pine nut mixture over the fish and garnish with sage.
Serves 4.*

CHAPTER FOUR
Meat and Poultry

Above: this evocative photograph from 1879 shows a family from Round Top, Texas, preparing sausages.

*B*eef has always been central to Tex-Mex cuisine, due in part to the reputation and enduring popularity given to it by the cowboy. Barbecued ribs and chilli stews are synonymous with Texas, and debate continues as to which is superior. Barbecuing beef over mesquite and concocting the perfect chilli are weighty issues for Texans and these dishes tend to overshadow the region's many other popular meat meals. Lamb, chicken and pork are all important meats, and both lamb and chicken are particularly suitable partners for fiery Tex-mex flavours. The astounding growth in the popularity of chicken is attributed to its nutritional quality and the influence of Mexico, where chicken has been the most popular meat since its introduction by the Spanish.

Minute Steaks with Taco Sauce

Southwestern Stir-Fry

East meets West in a dish that is lightning-fast to cook. Baby corn, traditionally Oriental, echoes the Southwestern love of corn.

450g/1lb sirloin or rump steak
2 cloves garlic, crushed
90ml/3 fl oz wine vinegar
90ml/3 fl oz oil
Pinch of sugar, salt and pepper
1 bay leaf
1 tbsp ground cumin
1 small red pepper, sliced
1 small green pepper, sliced
60g/2oz baby corn
4 spring onions, chopped
Oil for frying

RED SAUCE
60ml/2 fl oz oil
1 medium onion, finely chopped
1-2 green chillies, finely chopped
1-2 cloves garlic, crushed
8 fresh ripe tomatoes, peeled, seeded and chopped
6 sprigs fresh coriander
3 tbsps tomato purée

Slice the meat thinly across the grain. Combine in a plastic bag with the next 6 ingredients. Tie the bag and toss the ingredients inside

Texas is undoubtedly steak country. Here, the basic steak is given a Tex-Mex sauce to elevate it from the ordinary. Serve with rice or tortillas.

30g/1oz butter or margarine
2 tbsps oil
6 minute steaks
Salt and pepper
120g/4oz button mushrooms, left whole
Full quantity Taco Sauce recipe (see page 30)
Chopped parsley or coriander leaves

Heat the butter or margarine and oil together in a large frying pan. Season the steaks with salt and pepper and fry 2 or 3 at a time for 2-3 minutes on each side. Remove the steaks to a warm serving dish and add the mushrooms to the pan. Sauté over high heat to brown lightly, remove and keep warm. Drain most of the fat from the pan and pour in the taco sauce. Place over low heat until just bubbling. Spoon over the steaks. Top the steaks with the sautéed mushrooms and sprinkle over parsley or coriander before serving. Serves 6.

*to coat. Place in a bowl and leave about 4 hours.
Heat the oil for the sauce and cook the onion, chillies and garlic to soften but not brown. Add remaining sauce ingredients and cook about 15 minutes over gentle heat. Purée in a food processor until smooth. Heat a frying pan and add the meat in three batches, discarding the marinade. Cook to brown and set aside. Add about 2 tbsps of oil and cook the peppers about 2 minutes. Add the corn and onions and return the meat to the pan. Cook another minute and add the sauce. Cook to heat through and serve immediately. Serves 4.*

Above left: fortifications of the Presidio Santa Maria del Loreto de la Bahia, established in 1794, near Goliad.

Chilli Roja

Unlike authentic Mexican chilli, this recipe contains beans. There are countless different recipes for chilli, voted the Lone Star State's official dish, and at Terlinga there is even an annual Championship Chilli cook-off.

Chilli con Carne

This is the basic Tex-Mex chilli recipe – of which there are many versions and about which there are many arguments to be had! Chilli contests and cook-offs are a Texan phenomenon. Many cooks say no beans, others dispute over the type and quality of meat used and, of course, the amount of chilli powder used depends on your sense of bravado. Whatever the proportion of ingredients, chilli is good served with rice and topped with sour cream, chopped onion, grated cheese and diced avocado.

1 tbsp oil
450g/1lb ground beef
2 tsps ground cumin
2 tsps mild or hot chilli powder
Pinch of oregano
Salt, pepper and pinch sugar
¼ tsp garlic powder
2 tbsps flour
450g/1lb canned tomatoes
450g/1lb canned red kidney beans

Heat the oil in a large saucepan and brown the meat, breaking it up with a fork as it cooks. Sprinkle on the cumin, chilli powder, oregano, salt, pepper, sugar, garlic and flour. Cook, stirring frequently, over

4 tbsps oil
900g/2lbs stewing steak, cut into 2.5cm/1-inch pieces
1 large red onion, chopped
2 cloves garlic, crushed
2 red peppers, cut into 2.5cm/1-inch pieces
1-2 red chillies, seeded and finely chopped
3 tbsps mild chilli powder
1 tbsp cumin
1 tbsp paprika
750ml/26 fl oz beer, water or stock
225g/8oz canned tomatoes, puréed
2 tbsps tomato purée
225g/8oz canned red kidney beans, drained
Pinch of salt
6 ripe tomatoes, peeled, seeded and diced

Pour the oil into a large saucepan or flameproof casserole. When hot, brown the meat in small batches over moderately high heat for about 5 minutes per batch. Set aside the meat on a plate. Lower the heat and cook the onion, garlic, peppers and chillies for about 5 minutes. Add the chilli powder, cumin and paprika and cook for 1 minute further. Pour on the liquid and add the canned tomatoes, tomato purée and the meat. Cook slowly for about 1½-2 hours. Add the beans about 45 minutes before the end of cooking time. When the meat is completely tender, add salt to taste and serve garnished with the diced tomatoes. Serves 6-8.

medium heat for about 3 minutes. Add the tomatoes and their liquid and simmer 25-30 minutes. Drain the kidney beans and add just before serving. Heat through about 5 minutes. Serves 4.

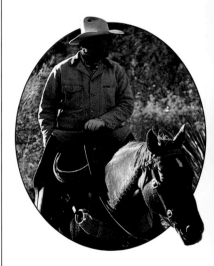

Above left: an early illustration of a Mexican household. Above: romanticized in numerous movies, the reality of life for a cowboy is a hard and often lonely existence.

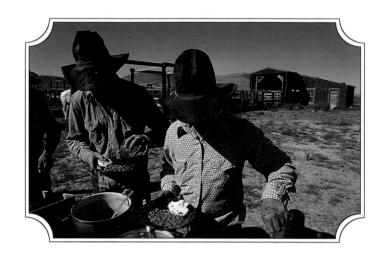

Mexican Chicken & Pepper Salad

A cool summer lunch for the scorching Tex-Mex summer is given character here by the addition of the local threesome: chilli, cayenne and paprika.

450g/1lb cooked chicken, cut in strips
140ml/¼ pint mayonnaise
140ml/¼ pint natural yogurt
1 tsp chilli powder
1 tsp paprika
Pinch of cayenne pepper
½ tsp tomato purée
1 tsp onion purée
1 green pepper, finely sliced
1 red pepper, finely sliced
180g/6oz frozen corn, defrosted
180g/6oz cooked long grain rice, to serve

Place the chicken strips in a large salad bowl. Mix the mayonnaise, yogurt, spices, tomato and onion purées together and leave to stand briefly for flavours to blend. Fold dressing into the chicken. Add the peppers and corn and mix gently until all the ingredients are coated with dressing. Place the rice on a serving dish and pile the salad into the centre. Serve immediately. Serves 6.

Above left: lunch on the 20,000-acre X Ranch near the Davis Mountains, Texas. Left: the Cathedral of Corpus Christi. Right: the Alamo Village, near Bracketville, built as a set for the movie The Alamo.

56

Albondigas (Meatballs)

Mexican Beef Patties

Adding refried beans to the ground beef in this Tex-Mex burger recipe adds flavour and interest, and also helps bind the meat together. Cumin, chilli and garlic are hallmarks of this region's cooking, and enliven these patties. They are good served with taco sauce, an avocado and tomato salad and warm flour tortillas.

1 onion, finely chopped
1 tbsp oil
340g/12oz ground beef
225g/8oz canned refried beans
4 tbsps breadcrumbs
½ tsp cumin
1 tsp chilli powder
1 clove garlic, crushed
Salt and pepper
1 egg, beaten
Flour to coat
Oil, for deep frying
Watercress, to garnish

Cook the onion in the oil until soft but not browned. Mix in the beef, beans, breadcrumbs, spices, garlic and seasoning and gradually add the egg until the mixture holds together well. Turn the mixture out onto a well-floured surface and divide into 8 pieces. Shape into

Taco sauce on these spicy meatballs gives this dish a double dose of Tex-Mex flavour, and they are well complemented with rice, refried beans or guacamole.

225g/8oz ground veal
225g/8oz ground beef
1 clove garlic, crushed
2 tbsps dry breadcrumbs
½ chilli, seeded and finely chopped
½ tsp ground cumin
Salt
1 egg, beaten
Flour, to coat
Oil for frying
Full quantity Taco Sauce recipe (see page 30)
2 spring onions, chopped

Mix together the veal, beef, garlic, breadcrumbs, chilli, cumin, salt and egg until well blended. Turn the mixture out onto a floured surface, divide into 16 equal pieces and shape the mixture into balls. Pour about 3 tablespoons of oil into a large frying pan and place over high heat. When the oil is hot, add the meatballs and fry for 5-10 minutes until brown on all sides. Turn frequently during cooking. Remove the meatballs and drain well on kitchen towels. Place in an ovenproof dish and pour over the taco sauce. Heat through in a preheated 180° C/350° F/Gas Mark 4 oven for 10 minutes. Sprinkle with chopped spring onions to serve. Serves 4.

even-sized patties with well-floured hands. Knead the pieces before shaping, if necessary, to make sure mixture holds together with no cracks. Coat lightly with flour and refrigerate until firm. Pour enough oil into a large pan to completely cover the patties. Fry 2 at a time until golden brown on all sides and completely cooked through. Remove from the oil and drain on kitchen towels. Arrange on a serving plate and garnish with watercress. Serves 4.

Above left: a Mexican wagon train loading up in Main Street, San Antonio.

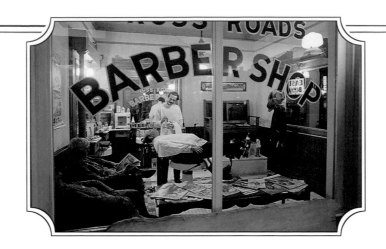

Spare Ribs in Chilli & Cream Sauce

Barbecued Ribs

Barbecued meats served with a sweet and spicy sauce are good eaten in the Texan/Mexican borderlands where warm, sultry evenings provide the perfect excuse for eating outside. Here, the meat is prepared in the oven for year-round convenience. Serve with warm tortillas and Spicy Rice and Beans.

2kg/4½lbs pork spare ribs

SAUCE
280ml/½ pint tomato ketchup
2 tsps mustard powder
4 tbsps Worcestershire sauce
2 tbsps vinegar
4 tbsps brown sugar
½ chilli, seeded and finely chopped
½ a small onion, finely chopped
4 tbsps water
Salt (if necessary)

Place the ribs in a roasting pan and cover with foil. Cook for 15 minutes at 220° C/425° F/Gas Mark 7. Meanwhile, combine all the sauce ingredients in a heavy-based pan and bring to the boil. Reduce heat and simmer for about 15 minutes. Reduce the oven temperature to 180° C/350° F/Gas Mark 4 and uncover the ribs. Pour

Cocoa and chillies seem unlikely partners, but it is authentic Tex-Mex, borrowed from Mexico where the cocoa bean has been used for centuries to add colour, depth and flavour. These ribs can be cooked on a barbecue for the last 30 minutes.

1kg 2¼ pounds spare ribs
1 tsp cocoa powder
1 tbsp flour
½ tsp cumin
½ tsp chilli powder
½ tsp dried oregano, crushed
Salt and pepper
280ml/½ pint warm water
2 tbsps thin honey
2 tbsps double cream
Lime wedges and watercress for garnish

Leave the ribs in whole slabs, put in a roasting pan and cook in a 200° C/400° F/Gas Mark 6 oven for 20-25 minutes, or until well browned. Drain off all the excess fat. Blend together the cocoa, flour, cumin, chilli powder, oregano, seasoning, water and honey and pour over the ribs. Lower the temperature to 180° C/350° F/Gas Mark 4 and cook ribs for a further 30 minutes, until the sauce has reduced and the ribs are tender. Cut the ribs into pieces and arrange on a serving dish. Pour the cream into the sauce in the roasting pan and place over moderate heat. Bring to the boil and pour over the ribs. Garnish with lime wedges and watercress.
Serves 4.

over the sauce and bake a further hour, basting frequently. Remove the ribs from the roasting pan and reserve the sauce. Slice the ribs into individual rib pieces, between the bones. Skim any fat from the surface of the sauce and serve the sauce separately. Serves 6.

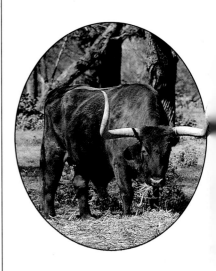

*Above left: the barber shop at the East Texas Oil Museum in Kilgore. The museum recreates many aspects of life in the oil boom days of the 1930s
Above: the much-prized Texas longhorn.*

Chicken with Red Peppers

The warm taste of roasted red peppers is typically Tex-Mex. Sage is a very common herb in the Southwestern United States. If unavailable fresh, substitute coriander or parsley leaves as a garnish.

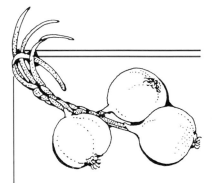

4 large red peppers
Oil
4 skinned and boned chicken breasts
Salt and pepper
1 clove garlic, finely chopped
3 tbsps white wine vinegar
2 spring onions, finely chopped
Sage leaves for garnish

Cut the peppers in half and remove the stems, cores and seeds. Flatten the peppers with the palm of your hand and brush the skin sides lightly with oil. Place the peppers skin side up on the rack of a preheated grill and cook about 5cm/2 inches away from the heat source until the skins are well blistered and charred. Wrap the peppers in a clean tea towel and allow them to stand until cool. Peel off the skins and discard. Cut the pepper flesh into thin strips and set aside.

Place the chicken breasts between two sheets of greaseproof paper and flatten by hitting with a rolling pin or meat mallet. Heat 1½ tablespoons of oil in a large frying pan. Season the chicken breasts on both sides and place in the hot oil. Cook 5 minutes, turn over and cook until tender and lightly browned. Remove the chicken and keep it warm. Add the pepper strips, garlic, vinegar and spring onions to the pan and cook briefly until the vinegar loses its strong aroma. Slice the chicken across the grain into 0.5cm/¼-inch thick slices and arrange on serving plates. Spoon the pan juices over the chicken. Arrange the pepper mixture with the chicken and garnish with the sage leaves. Serves 4.

Right: although the Texan economy is now dominated by oil and computers, cattle ranching remains a vital social and economic force.

Leg of Lamb with Chilli Sauce

Here familiar Tex-Mex spices – cayenne, cumin and paprika – are mixed with cocoa, which is used not as a sweetening but as a seasoning, as was traditional in pre-Columbian Mexico. You do not notice a chocolate flavour in this dish, the cocoa rather adds a depth and richness to the sauce.

1kg/2¼-pound leg of lamb

MARINADE
1 tsp cocoa powder
¼ tsp cayenne pepper
½ tsp ground cumin
½ tsp paprika
½ tsp ground oregano
140ml/¼ pint water
140ml/¼ pint orange juice
140ml/¼ pint red wine
1 clove of garlic, crushed
2 tbsps brown sugar
Pinch of salt
1 tbsp cornflour
Orange slices and coriander, to garnish

If the lamb has a lot of surface fat, trim with a sharp knife. If possible, remove the paper-thin skin on the outside of the lamb. Place lamb in a shallow dish. Mix together the marinade ingredients, except cornflour, and pour over the lamb, turning it well to coat completely.

Cover and refrigerate for 12–24 hours, turning occasionally.
Drain the lamb, reserving the marinade, and place in a roasting pan. Cook in a preheated 180° C/350° F/Gas Mark 4 oven for about 2 hours until meat is cooked according to taste. Baste occasionally with the marinade and pan juices. Remove lamb to a serving dish and keep warm. Skim the fat from the roasting pan and discard. Pour remaining marinade into the pan juices in the roasting pan and bring to the boil, stirring to loosen the sediment. Mix cornflour with a small amount of water and add some of the liquid from the roasting pan. Gradually stir cornflour mixture into the pan and bring back to the boil. Cook, stirring constantly, until thickened and clear. Add more orange juice, wine or water as necessary. Garnish the lamb with orange slices and sprigs of coriander. Pour over some of the sauce and serve the rest separately. Serves 4.

Above: Sidbury House in Heritage Park, a plaza of restored and relocated turn-of-the-century houses in Corpus Christi.

64

Mexican Kebabs

These delicious Tex-Mex kebabs marry Texan barbecue cooking with the ancient Mexican spice combination of bitter cocoa and biting chillies.

450g/1lb pork or lamb, cubed
120g/4oz large button mushrooms, left whole
8 bay leaves
1 tsp cocoa powder
2 tsps chilli powder
¼ tsp garlic powder
½ tsp dried marjoram
Salt and pepper
90ml/3 fl oz oil
2 medium onions, quartered
180g/6oz cooked rice, to serve
½ quantity Taco Sauce recipe (see page 30)

Place meat and mushrooms in a bowl. Add the bay leaves, cocoa, chilli powder, garlic powder, marjoram and seasoning to the oil and stir into the meat and mushrooms to coat. Cover the bowl and leave to marinate at least 6 hours, preferably overnight. Remove meat, mushrooms and bay leaves from the marinade and reserve it. Thread onto skewers, alternating meat, onions, mushrooms and bay leaves. Place under a preheated grill for 15-20 minutes, turning frequently until cooked. If using pork, the meat must be thoroughly cooked and not served pink. Baste with reserved marinade. Mix hot rice with taco sauce and spoon onto a warm serving dish. Place the kebabs on top of the rice to serve. Serves 4.

Above left: only the birds disturb the peace at Monahans Sandhills State Park, a hazardous barrier that once hampered many wagon trains heading across the state.
Above: dipping sheep in Southwest Texas. Left: the old post office near Hot Springs, Big Bend National Park.

Barbecued Pork Stew

Peppers, chilli powder and Tabasco sauce turn this pork stew into a really spicy Tex-Mex dish. Serve with warm tortillas and Spicy Rice and Beans.

Chilli Verde

This is a green version of the Texan classic 'bowl of red'. Generally in Tex-Mex cooking a chilli has come to mean a meat and chilli stew. There are many variations and Texan cooks pride themselves on their own chilli recipes. Serve this for lunch or a light supper with warm tortillas.

Oil
900g/2lbs lean pork, cut into
2.5cm/1-inch pieces
3 green peppers, cut into
2.5cm/1-inch pieces
1-2 green chillies, seeded and
finely chopped
1 small bunch spring onions,
chopped
2 cloves garlic, crushed
2 tsps ground cumin
2 tsps chopped fresh oregano
3 tbsps chopped fresh coriander
1 bay leaf
750ml/26 fl oz beer, water or
chicken stock
225g/8oz canned
chickpeas, drained
1½ tbsps cornflour mixed with
3 tbsps cold water (optional)
Salt
1 large ripe avocado, diced
1 tbsp lime juice

Oil
900g/2lbs pork shoulder, cut in 5cm/2-inch cubes
2 medium onions, cut in 5cm/2-inch pieces
1 large green pepper, cut in 5cm/2-inch pieces
1 tbsp chilli powder
2 cloves garlic, crushed
450g/1lb canned tomatoes
3 tbsps tomato purée
1 tbsp Worcestershire sauce
140ml/¼ pint water or beef stock
2 tbsps cider vinegar
1 bay leaf
½ tsp dried oregano
Salt and a few drops Tabasco sauce

Heat about 2 tablespoons of oil in a large heavy-based saucepan. When hot, add the pork cubes in two batches. Brown over high heat for about 5 minutes per batch. Remove to a plate. Add more oil if necessary and cook the onions and peppers to soften slightly. Add the chilli powder and garlic and cook 1 minute more. Add the tomatoes, their juice and the tomato purée. Stir in the Worcestershire sauce, water or stock, and vinegar, breaking up the tomatoes slightly. Add bay leaf, oregano and salt. Bring the mixture to the boil, cover, and then cook slowly for about 1½ hours. When the meat is completely tender, skim any fat from the surface of the sauce, remove the bay leaf and add a few drops of Tabasco sauce to taste. Adjust salt and serve. Serves 4.

Heat 4 tablespoons of oil in a large flameproof casserole and lightly brown the pork cubes over high heat. Lower the heat, add the peppers and cook to soften slightly. Add the chillies, onions, garlic and cumin and cook for 2 minutes. Add the herbs and liquid and reduce the heat. Simmer, covered, 1-1½ hours or until the meat is tender. Add the chickpeas during the last 45 minutes. If necessary, thicken with the cornflour, stirring constantly after adding until the liquid thickens and clears. Add salt to taste and remove the bay leaf. Toss the avocado in lime juice and sprinkle over the top of the chilli to serve. Serves 6-8.

Above left: futuristic office blocks are in marked contrast to the 'pioneer village' in Dallas' Old City Park.

CHAPTER FIVE
Snacks and Side dishes

Above: a cowboy moves a herd of working horses on to the next camp on the ranch.

*T*ex-Mex cooking features many lively snacks and side dishes, from the traditional favourites such as refried beans, to spicy sophisticated salads. Beans were once an invaluable part of the diet of cattlemen who ate red, broad beans or pinto beans stewed into an unappetizing, if nutritious, mush and served with cornbread or biscuits. A more recent rise in status has been accorded to salads. At one time the only sight of a salad would have been sprinkled over the top of tacos, but today's health-conscious cooks have devised many delicious salads using some favourite Tex-Mex ingredients, but adding some lighter tastes such as endive and pine nuts.

Refried Beans

This is a classic Mexican and Tex-Mex dish, both in its own right served with tortillas – as here – or as an accompaniment to poultry, meat or vegetable recipes.

Tostadas

Tex-Mex cooking encompasses a great variety of 'finger foods', such as these tostadas. The Tex-Mex cook has great flexibility to experiment with different fillings and toppings, and the number of chillies used!

450g/1lb ground beef or pork
2 tsps oil
2 tsps chilli powder
1 tsp ground cumin
1 tsp ground coriander
340g/12oz refried beans
12 tostada shells

TOPPINGS
Shredded lettuce
Grated Cheddar cheese
Tomatoes, seeded and chopped
Soured cream
Olives
Cooked prawns
Spring onions, chopped
Taco Sauce (see page 30)

Cook the meat in the oil in a frying pan, breaking up the meat with a fork as it cooks. Sprinkle on the spices and cook quickly to brown.

225g/8oz dried pinto beans
Water, to cover
1 bay leaf
90ml/3 fl oz oil
Salt and pepper
Grated mild cheese
Shredded lettuce
Tortillas

Soak the beans overnight. Change the water, add the bay leaf and bring to the boil. Cover and simmer about 2 hours, or until the beans are completely tender. Alternatively, bring the beans to the boil in cold water and then allow to boil rapidly for 10 minutes. Cover and leave to stand for 1 hour. Change the water and then continue with the recipe. Drain the beans and reserve a small amount of the cooking liquid. Discard bay leaf. Heat the oil in a heavy frying pan. Add the beans and, as they fry, mash them with the back of a spoon. Do not overmash – about a third of the beans should stay whole. Season to taste. Smooth out the beans in the pan and cook until the bottom is set but not browned. Turn the beans over and cook the other side. Top with the cheese and cook the beans until the cheese melts. Serve with finely shredded lettuce and tortillas, either warm or cut in triangles and deep-fried until crisp. Serves 6-8.

Heat the beans. Place the tostada shells on a baking sheet and heat 2-3 minutes in a moderate oven. Spread 1-2 tablespoons of the beans on each tostada shell. Top each shell with some of the beef mixture. Vary the topping ingredients and serve. Serves 12.

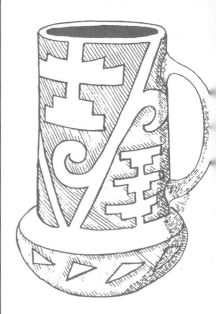

Above left: an early illustration of a wealthy household in Monterey, once considered the social centre of Northern Mexico. Right: the rustic simplicity of a ranch dining room.

Spicy Rice and Beans

Rice and beans are natural Tex-Mex partners, especially when spiced with peppers, cumin and coriander. This can be served with warm tortillas and a salad, or as a side dish with enchiladas, meat or poultry.

Above left: Guadalupe Mountains National Park. Left: Old Nacodoches University, built in 1858.

4 tbsps oil
225g/8oz long grain rice
1 onion, finely chopped
1 green pepper, chopped
1 tsp each ground cumin and coriander
1-2 tsps Tabasco
Salt
1 litre/1¾ pints vegetable stock
450g/1lb canned red kidney beans, drained and rinsed
450g/1lb tomatoes, coarsely chopped and drained
Chopped parsley

Heat the oil in a large, deep saucepan. Add the rice and cook until just turning opaque. Add the onion, pepper, cumin and coriander. Cook gently for a further 2 minutes. Add the Tabasco, salt, stock and beans and bring to the boil. Cover and cook about 45 minutes, or until the rice is tender and most of the liquid is absorbed. Remove from the heat and add the tomatoes, stirring them in gently. Leave to stand, covered, for 5 minutes. Fluff up the mixture with a fork and sprinkle with parsley to serve. Serves 6-8.

PARSLEY

Salad Huevos Rancheros

Originally a cowboy dish consisting of just chorizo and spring onions, this more sophisticated version is now a Tex-Mex appetizer.

1 large red pepper, roasted (see Chicken with Red
Peppers page 62)
1 chorizo sausage
4 heads chicory
2 small courgettes, cut into matchstick pieces
1 small jicama root, cut into matchstick pieces (optional)
2-3 spring onions, shredded
4 tbsps pine nuts
4 eggs
1 tsp chopped fresh coriander

DRESSING
90ml/3 fl oz oil
2 tbsps lime juice
Dash of Tabasco
Salt and pinch of sugar

Prepare the roasted pepper and cut it into thin strips. Bring a pan of water to the boil, add the chorizo and simmer for about 8 minutes until tender. Peel the casing off the chorizo while warm and cut the meat into thin strips. Separate the leaves of the chicory and slice or leave whole if small. Bring water to the boil and blanch the courgette and jicama strips for 1 minute. Rinse under cold water until completely cool and leave to drain.

Combine with the chicory and spring onion. Add the strips of chorizo and set aside. Toast the pine nuts in a moderate oven until golden brown – about 5 minutes. Bring at least 5cm/2 inches of water to the boil in a sauté pan. Turn down the heat to simmering. Break an egg onto a saucer or into a cup. Stir the water to make a whirlpool and then carefully pour the egg into the centre, keeping the saucer or cup close to the level of the water. When the water stops swirling and the white begins to set, gently move the egg over to the side and repeat with each remaining egg. Cook the eggs until the whites are completely set, but the yolks are still soft. Remove the eggs from the water with a draining spoon and place them immediately into a bowl of cold water.
Mix the dressing ingredients together and pour half over the vegetables and sausage. Toss to coat. Arrange the mixture on individual plates in the shape of nests. Remove the eggs from the cold water with the draining spoon and hold them over a towel for a few minutes to drain completely. Place one egg in the middle of each nest. Spoon the remaining dressing over each egg, sprinkle over the pine nuts and garnish the yolk with chopped coriander. Serves 4.

Above: a scene from 1885 of the historic fountain in the Plaza Santo Domingo, Mexico City. Right: the largest park in the Lone Star State, Big Bend National Park covers more than 700,000 acres and is a haven for backpackers and nature lovers.

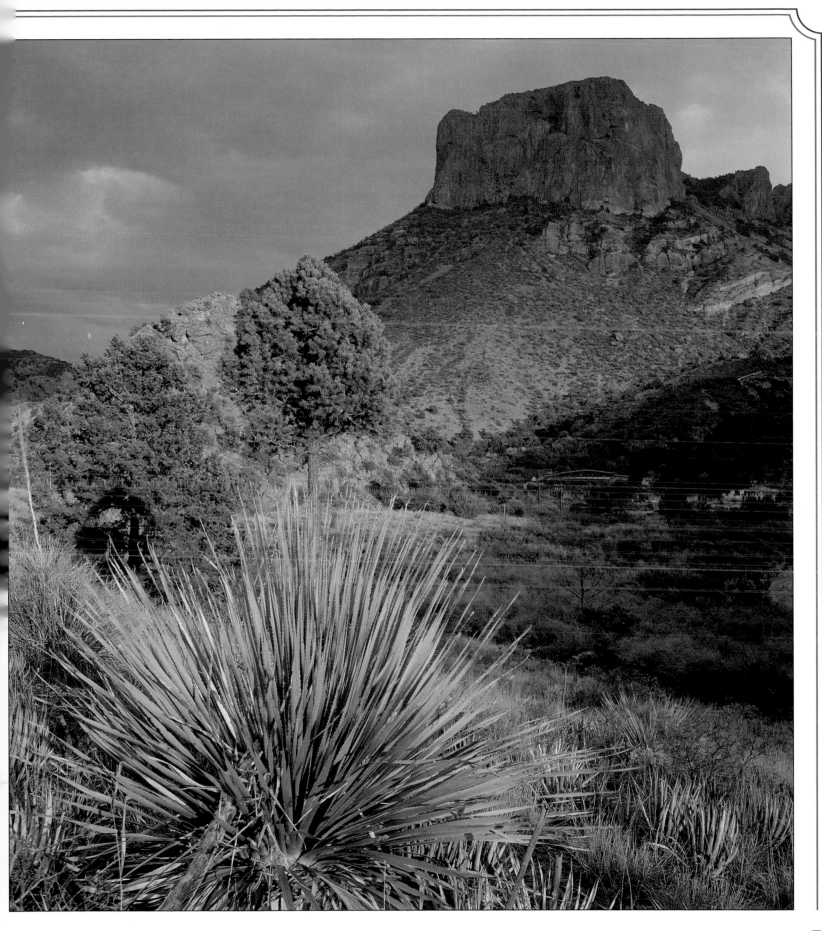

Churros

These fritters can be either sweet or savoury. Either way, they're a treat with a Mexican influence.

BASIC DOUGH
225ml/8 fl oz water
45g/1½oz butter or margarine
Pinch of salt
120g/4oz plain flour
6 tbsps cornmeal
2 eggs
Oil for deep frying

SAVOURY INGREDIENTS
2 tbsps finely grated cheese
2 chillies, seeded and finely chopped
Parmesan cheese (optional)

SWEET INGREDIENTS
60g/2oz sugar
1 tbsp cocoa powder
1 tsp ground cinnamon
Icing sugar (optional)

Combine the water, butter or margarine and salt in a heavy-based saucepan. If making sweet churros, add sugar as well. Cook over medium heat until the butter or margarine melts. Immediately stir in the flour and cornmeal. Keeping the pan over medium heat, stir until the mixture pulls away from the sides of the pan and forms a ball. Take off the heat and cool slightly. Add the eggs one at a time, beating vigorously in between each addition. It may not be necessary to add all the egg. Beat until the mixture is smooth and shiny and thick enough to pipe. Add the cheese and chillies or the cocoa and cinnamon with the eggs. Spoon the mixture into a pastry bag fitted with a star nozzle.

Heat the oil in a deep-fat fryer or deep saucepan to a depth of at least 10cm/4 inches. Pipe the dough into the oil in 25cm/10-inch strips and fry until golden brown, about 3 minutes per side. As the churros cook in the hot fat, they will curl into different shapes. Drain on kitchen towels and sprinkle the savoury churros with Parmesan cheese and the sweet with icing sugar, if desired. Serve warm. Makes 12-14.

Above: this 1925 photograph shows a young resident of San Antonio baking a cake for needy fellow citizens.

Moyettes

This is a Tex-Mex brunch dish which can be prepared in advance and heated through just before serving.

4 crusty rolls
30g/1oz butter or margarine
225g/8oz canned refried beans
2 spring onions, chopped
4 tbsps grated Tilsit cheese

Cut the rolls in half and remove some of the inside. Spread the butter on both sides of the rolls. Fill the rolls with the refried beans. Sprinkle with the spring onion and top with the grated cheese. Place the rolls on a baking sheet and cook in a preheated 160° C/325° F/Gas Mark 3 oven for 15-20 minutes, or until the cheese has melted and the beans are hot. Serve immediately.
Serves 4.

Nachos

These make excellent Tex-Mex cocktail savouries. It is best to make them at the last minute as tortilla chips become soggy if topped too soon before serving.

1 packet round tortilla chips
1 large can refried beans
Full quantity Taco Sauce recipe (see page 30)
1 can Jalapeño bean dip
8-10 cherry tomatoes, sliced
140ml/¼ pint soured cream or plain yogurt
Sliced black and stuffed green olives
Grated Cheddar cheese

TACO FILLING
2 tsps oil
225g/8oz ground beef
2 tsps chilli powder
Pinch of ground coriander
Pinch of cayenne pepper
Salt and pepper

Prepare taco filling as for Tacos recipe. Top half of the tortilla chips with refried beans and half with beef taco filling. Place a spoonful of taco sauce on the bean-topped chips and Jalapeño bean dip in the beef-topped chips. Top the tortilla chips with tomatoes, soured cream or yogurt, olives or cheese in any desired combination, and serve.
Serves 8-10.

Above left: San Antonio market place in 1883. Above: the Spanish Governor's Palace in San Antonio, built in 1749, once housed the officials of the Spanish Province of Texas.

Denver Omelette

This is a good one-pan cowboy recipe. If prepared like scrambled eggs, the mixture can double as a tortilla filling.

4 rashers bacon, diced
½ small onion, chopped
½ small green pepper, chopped
1 tomato, seeded and diced
3 eggs, beaten
Salt and pepper
1 tbsp grated cheese
Dash of Tabasco (optional)
Chopped parsley, to garnish

Heat a medium-size frying or omelette pan. Add the bacon and sauté slowly until the fat is rendered. Turn up the heat and cook until the bacon begins to brown and crisp. Add the onion and pepper and cook to soften and finish off the bacon. Mix the tomato with the eggs, salt, pepper, cheese, and Tabasco, if using. Pour into the pan and stir once or twice with a fork to mix all the ingredients. Cook until lightly browned on the underside. Place under a pre-heated grill and cook the top quickly until brown and slightly puffy. Sprinkle with parsley, cut into wedges and serve immediately. Serves 2.

Above left: the Swedish Log Cabin in Zilker Park, Austin. Above: the spectacular view across Chisos Basin, in Big Bend National Park.

CHAPTER SIX
Desserts

*Above: the authentically-furnished Spanish
Governor's Palace in San Antonio, built in 1749.*

*D*esserts are an important feature of any
Tex-mex meal as they help to extinguish
the heat of a spicy main course with a cool or sweet
finale. Chocolate flans are one of the most popular
desserts and it is, in fact, the Aztecs who are credited
with popularising the cocoa bean and turning it into
an extremely strong chocolate drink, although it was
a long time before it became the chocolate we know
and love today. Other popular desserts include
watermelon, fresh fruit salads, syrup-poached fruit
and, of course, ice creams and fruit ices. All of these
provide the perfect method for dusting down and
refreshing the taste buds.

Black Bottom Ice Cream Pie

Fruit Empanadas

Tortillas when stuffed and deep-fried become empanadas.

Full quantity Tortilla recipe (see page 26)
Oil for deep frying
10 ripe fresh apricots, halved and pitted, or 450g/1lb canned apricots, well drained
450g/1lb cream cheese
Icing sugar

Prepare the tortilla dough, roll out into 10 tortillas but do not pre-cook. Heat oil in a deep saucepan, sauté pan or deep-fat fryer to a depth of at least 5cm/2 inches. Oil should reach a temperature of 190° C/375° F. Cut the apricots into quarters and the cheese into 10 even pieces. Place one piece of cheese and an even amount of apricots on the lower half of each tortilla. Fold over the upper half and seal the edges. Crimp tightly into a decorative pattern. Fry one empanada at a time until golden on both sides. Baste the upper side frequently with oil to make the tortilla dough puffy. Drain well on kitchen towels and serve warm, sprinkled with icing sugar.

This area of border cooking is all about strong, positive flavours and indulgence, which is easy when local products include coffee, cocoa, coconut and rum.

12 Digestive biscuits, crushed
90g/3oz butter, melted
120g/4oz flaked coconut
60g/2oz plain chocolate, melted
840ml/1½ pints coffee ice cream
Dark rum (optional)

Crush biscuits with a rolling pin. Mix with melted butter. Press into a 21cm/8½-inch deep spring form tin. Chill thoroughly in the refrigerator. Meanwhile, combine 4 tablespoons of the coconut with the melted chocolate. When cooled but not solidified, add about a quarter of the coffee ice cream, mixing well. Spread the mixture on the base of the crust and freeze until firm. Soften the remaining ice cream with an electric mixer or food processor and spread over the chocolate-coconut layer. Re-freeze until firm. Toast the remaining coconut in a moderate oven, stirring frequently until pale golden brown. Allow to cool completely. Remove the pie from the freezer and leave in the refrigerator 30 minutes before serving. Push up the base of the tin and place the pie on a serving plate. Sprinkle the top with toasted coconut. Cut into wedges and drizzle with rum before serving.

Mango Fool

Mangoes, laced with ginger and lime, offer a wonderful taste of Mexico and a soothing coolness ideal to placate the palate following a fiery Texan chilli.

2 ripe mangoes
1 small piece root ginger, peeled and shredded
120g/4oz icing sugar, sieved
Juice of ½ a lime
280ml/½ pint double cream

Cut the mangoes in half, cutting around the stone. Scoop out the pulp into a blender or food processor. Reserve two slices. Add the ginger, icing sugar and lime juice and purée in the blender or food processor until smooth. Whip the cream until soft peaks form and fold into the mango purée. Divide the mixture between 6 glass serving dishes and refrigerate for 1 hour before serving. Cut the reserved mango slices into 6 smaller slices or pieces and decorate the fools. Serves 6.

Above left: the hectic days following the discovery of the huge East Texas Oil Field in 1930 are recreated at the Oil Museum in Kilgore.

Tropical Fruit Salad

Guava Mint Sorbet

The stimulating combination of guava and mint is very typical of the exotic Tex-Mex range of piquant tastes.

180g/6oz sugar
280ml/½ pint water
4 ripe guavas
2 tbsps chopped fresh mint
Juice of 1 lime
1 egg white
Fresh mint leaves, to decorate

Combine the sugar and water in a heavy-based saucepan and bring slowly to the boil to dissolve the sugar. When the mixture is a clear syrup, boil rapidly for 30 seconds. Allow to cool to room temperature and then chill in the refrigerator. Cut the guavas in half and scoop out the pulp. Discard the peels and seeds and purée the fruit until smooth. Add the mint and combine with cold syrup. Add lime juice until the right balance of sweetness is reached. Pour the mixture into a shallow container and freeze until slushy. Process again to break up ice crystals and then freeze until firm. Whip the egg white until stiff but not dry. Process the sorbet again and when smooth, add

Tex-Mex cooking offers a feast of succulent fruits which continue the theme of strong vibrant flavours so characteristic of this part of the world. A splash of tequila adds sophistication and an even greater authenticity to this fruit salad.

½ cantaloupe or honeydew melon, cubed or made into balls
½ small fresh pineapple, peeled, cored and cubed or sliced
120g/4oz fresh strawberries, hulled and halved (leave whole, if small)
1 mango, peeled and sliced or cubed
225g/8oz watermelon, seeded and cubed
120g/4oz guava or papaya, peeled and cubed
2 oranges, peeled and segmented
1 prickly pear, peeled and sliced (optional)
120g/4oz sugar
140ml/¼ pint water
Grated rind and juice of 1 lemon
2 tbsps chopped pecans, to garnish (optional)

Mix the prepared fruit together in a bowl. Dissolve the sugar in the water over gentle heat and when the mixture is no longer grainy, leave it to cool completely. Add lemon rind and juice to the sugar syrup and pour over the prepared fruit. Refrigerate well before serving. Sprinkle with chopped nuts, if desired. Serves 6.

the egg white. Mix once or twice and then freeze again until firm. Remove from the freezer 15 minutes before serving and keep in the refrigerator. Scoop out and garnish each serving with mint. Makes 850ml/1½ pints.

Above left: the Law Office in Sam Houston Memorial Park, Huntsville. Right: a fascinating recreation of a 1930s store.

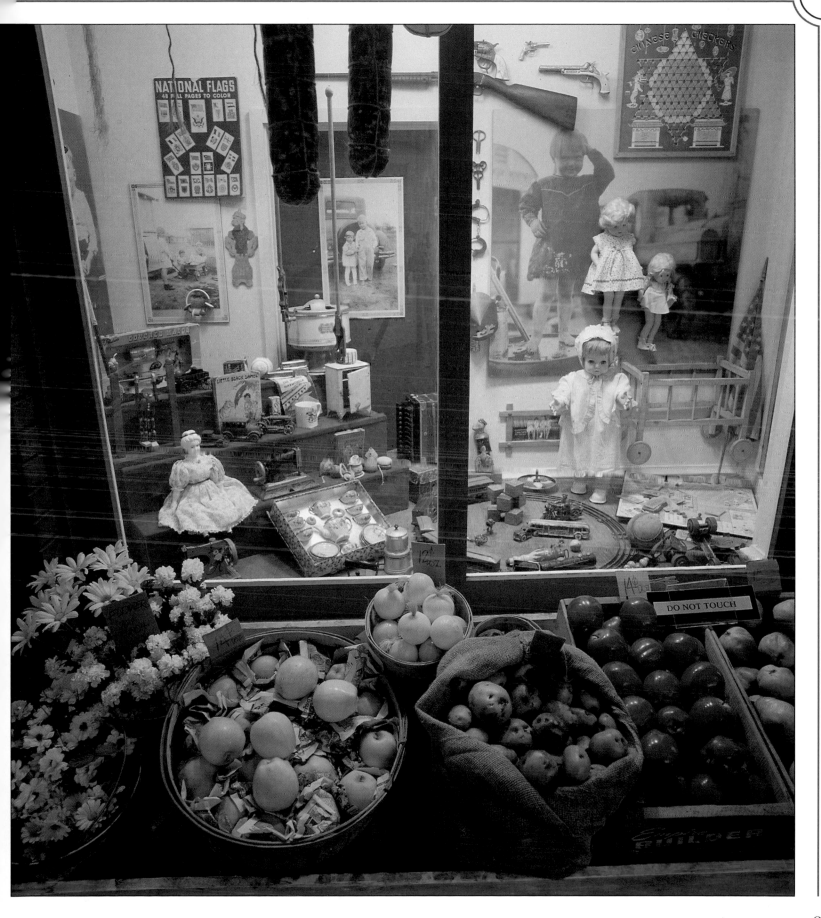

Mexican Chocolate Flan

Flan in Mexico means a custard mould. Cocoa beans, an important Tex-Mex ingredient, are native to southern Mexico and were imported by the Aztecs into central Mexico where they were so valued they were used as a form of currency, and later to make chocolate. Cinnamon, which is combined with chocolate here, is also a traditional Tex-Mex flavour.

120g/4oz sugar
2 tbsps water
Juice of ½ a lemon
60g/2oz plain chocolate
280ml/½ pint milk
1 cinnamon stick
2 whole eggs
2 egg yolks
4 tbsps sugar

Combine the first amount of sugar with the water and lemon juice in a small, heavy-based saucepan. Cook over gentle heat until the sugar starts to dissolve. Swirl the pan from time to time, but don't stir. Once the sugar liquifies, bring the syrup to the boil and cook until golden brown. While preparing the syrup, heat 4 ramekins in a 180° C/350° F/Gas Mark 4 oven. When the syrup is ready, pour into the ramekins and swirl to coat the sides and base evenly. Leave to cool at room temperature.
Chop the chocolate into small pieces and heat with the milk and cinnamon, stirring occasionally to help the chocolate dissolve. Whisk the whole eggs and the yolks together with the remaining sugar until slightly frothy. Gradually whisk in the chocolate milk. Remove the cinnamon stick. Pour the chocolate custard carefully into the ramekins and place them in a roasting pan of hand-hot water. Place the roasting pan in the oven and bake the custards until just slightly wobbly in the centre – about 20-30 minutes. Cool at room temperature and refrigerate for several hours or overnight before serving. Loosen custards carefully from the sides of the dishes and invert onto serving plates. Shake to allow custards to drop out. Serves 4.

Frozen Lime and Blueberry Cream

Blueberries are the traditional ingredient in this recipe, but if they are unavailable you can substitute blackcurrants.

Juice and rind of 4 limes
Water
225g/8oz sugar
120g/4oz blueberries
3 egg whites
280ml/½ pint double cream, whipped

Measure the lime juice and make up to 90ml/3 fl oz with water if necessary. Combine with the sugar in a heavy-based pan and bring to the boil slowly to dissolve the sugar. When the mixture forms a clear syrup, boil rapidly to 130° C/250° F on a candy thermometer. Meanwhile, combine the blueberries with about 4 tablespoons water in a small saucepan. Bring to the boil and then simmer, covered, until very soft. Purée, sieve to remove the seeds and skin, and set aside to cool. Whisk the egg whites until stiff but not dry and then pour on the hot sugar syrup in a steady stream, beating constantly. Add the lime rind and allow to cool. When cold, fold in the whipped cream. Pour in the purée and marble through the mixture with a rubber spatula. Do not over-fold. Pour the mixture into a lightly-oiled mould or bowl and freeze until firm. To serve, dip the mould for about 10 seconds in hot water. Place a plate over the bottom of the mould, invert and shake to turn out. Decorate with extra whipped cream, blueberries or lime slices. Serves 6.

Chocolate Cinnamon Monkey Bread

Cocoa and cinnamon both appear in early accounts of Mexican cooking, and indeed when these ingredients were roasted together with chillies this was the first way in which cocoa appears to have been eaten.

DOUGH
1 tbsp sugar
1 envelope dry yeast
60ml/2 fl oz warm water
340-400g/12-14oz strong flour
90g/3oz sugar
Pinch of salt
75g/2½oz butter, softened
5 eggs

TOPPING
225g/8oz sugar
2 tsps cinnamon
2 tsps cocoa powder
120g/4oz finely chopped pecans
120g/4oz butter, melted

Sprinkle 1 tablespoon sugar and the yeast on top of the water and leave it in a warm place until foaming. Sift 340g/12oz flour into a bowl and add the sugar and salt. Rub in the butter until completely blended. Add 2 eggs and the yeast mixture, mixing in well. Add the remaining eggs one at a time until the mixture forms a soft, spongy dough. Add remaining flour as necessary.

Knead for 10 minutes on a lightly floured surface until smooth and elastic. Place the dough in a greased bowl and turn over to grease all the surfaces. Cover loosely and put in a warm place. Leave to stand for 1-1½ hours or until doubled in bulk.

Butter a ring mould liberally. Knock the dough down and knead it again for about 5 minutes. Shape into balls about 5cm/2 inches in diameter. Mix the topping ingredients together except for the melted butter. Roll the dough balls in the butter and then in the sugar mixture. Place a layer of dough balls in the bottom of the mould and continue until all the dough and topping has been used. Cover and allow to rise again about 15 minutes. Bake in a pre-heated 180°C/350°F/Gas Mark 4 oven for about 45-50 minutes. Loosen from the pan and turn out while still warm. Pull the bread apart to serve in individual pieces rather than slicing it.

Above: southwest Texas is perfect hiking country noted for its spectacular views and varied plant and animal life.

Index

Acknowledgements

The publishers would like to thank the following organizations and individuals
for contributing to the book: The Society of Texan Cultures, San Antonio, Texas;
San Antonio Conservation Society; U.T. The Institute of Texan Cultures, The San
Antonio Light Collection; Zeva Olebaum; Sue Philpot; Louisa Vernay